Gwynne's Grammar

Gwynne's Grammar

THE ULTIMATE INTRODUCTION
TO GRAMMAR AND THE WRITING
OF GOOD ENGLISH

Definitions, explanations and illustrations
of the parts of speech, and of the other
most important technical terms of grammar.
Incorporating Strunk's Guide to Style
explaining how to write well and
the main pitfalls to avoid.

N. M. Gwynne, M.A. (Oxon.)

ALFRED A. KNOPF   NEW YORK   2014

THIS IS A BORZOI BOOK
PUBLISHED BY ALFRED A. KNOPF

Copyright © 2013, 2014 by N. M. Gwynne

www.aaknopf.com

Knopf, Borzoi Books, and the colophon are registered
trademarks of Random House LLC.

Originally published in slightly different form
by Ebury Press, an imprint of Ebury Publishing,
a Random House Group company, London, in 2013.

Library of Congress Cataloging-in-Publication Data
Gwynne, N. M.
Gwynne's grammar : the ultimate introduction
to grammar and the writing of good English /
N.M. Gwynne. — First American Edition.
pages   cm
ISBN 978-0-385-35293-2 (hardback)
ISBN 978-0-385-35294-9 (eBook)
1. English language—Grammar.   2. English language—
Punctuation.   3. English language—Rhetoric.
I. Title.   II. Title: Grammar.   III. Title: The ultimate
introduction to grammar and the writing of good English.
PE1106.G89 2014
425—dc23   2014019245

Jacket design by Oliver Munday

Manufactured in the United States of America
First American Edition

To those pupils of mine in various parts of the world,
of ages ranging from two years old right up to elderly adulthood,
and in many cases to their parents and even grandparents as well,
all of whom between them are primarily responsible
for this book — or, rather, book's — coming into existence

Contents

Preface   *ix*

PART I · GWYNNE'S GRAMMAR

1. This Is a Serious Business   3
2. A Note of Encouragement   5
3. Further Encouragement   11
4. Does Prescriptiveness *Really* Belong to Grammar?   15
5. Still Introductory   23
6. Parts of Speech   31
7. The Most Important Syntax Basics   67
8. Punctuation   84
9. Putting What Is Being Learnt into Practice   101
10. The Grammar of Verse-Writing   106

PART II · STRUNK ON STYLE

Foreword by N. M. Gwynne   135
1. Introductory   141
2. Elementary Rules of Usage   143
3. Elementary Principles of Composition   155

4. A Few Matters of Form   180
5. Words and Expressions Commonly Misused   184

PART III · APPENDICES: SOME USEFUL LISTS

1. Inventory of Definitions of Grammatical Terms   199
2. The Irregular Verbs   210
3. Special Prepositions Needed by Particular Words   218
4. The Formation of Plurals   224

Further Reading (by N. M. Gwynne)   229
Acknowledgements   237
Index   239

Preface

Much more than is customary, this Preface is intrinsic to a proper understanding of the rest of this book and to how to make the best possible use of it. The reader is urged to read it with some care.

I can say with complete safety that what you have in your hands is a thoroughly *practical* little book. It owes that feature to a number of remarkable circumstances.

The first is the manner in which it came into existence. For many years now, I have been teaching, at one time or another, most of the academic subjects but principally Latin. Thanks to the Internet, I have been doing this largely while sitting at home—remarkably, within seconds of a class starting, it is as though we are in the same classroom together.

My pupils' ages have ranged from two years old to over seventy. Of the younger ones, some have been homeschooled, and some I have given classes to just before or after school, in parts of the world ranging from India in one direction, through Europe, to the west coast of the United States in the other. I have even been employed by Selfridges (one of the two most famous department stores in London, Harrods being the other) to give a series of once-a-week lectures on English grammar, most of them two hours long, to all comers in the store's Ultralounge.

In every case, I have been having to tackle English grammar with my pupils, either because it has been largely forgotten by my older pupils or because it has been ignored, most often completely, in the schools that my younger pupils attend or have attended. I have had to do this simply in order to make it possible to teach the other subjects satisfactorily.

Enter now the publisher of the original edition of this book, Mr. Tom Hodgkinson, the father in one of "my" families of pupils. From the time that I started teaching his children after school hours, he would often sit in on the classes, as I very much encourage parents, and even grandparents and other family members, to do when they can. Himself an experienced journalist, he was endlessly interested by the English grammar I was teaching his children—so much so that he eventually came up with the suggestion that I should put together what I had been teaching into a small book which he would publish, and which we could be confident would be useful and helpful. He even chose its two-word title.

In spite of very little advertising other than by word of mouth, the first edition exhausted its print run with encouraging speed, as did two subsequent editions, each of them incorporating additional material arising from questions raised and comments made by my pupils, and by others of all ages who have read this book, including schoolteachers of the highest seniority.

The next development was that Mr. Jake Lingwood of Ebury Press, of the Random House Group, noticed the book in a catalogue, and approached Mr. Hodgkinson and me, with the suggestion that a well-designed cover and the sort of promotion that a large publishing company could offer might bring the book to a much wider readership. The result of the new partnership that emerged was, to me at least, astonishing. At once the Ebury edition reached the top ten hardback best sellers in England, and even number one in some lists, and there it stayed for about five months.

Now comes this book's introduction to America, courtesy of Alfred A. Knopf, and it is safe to say that what you are now reading is tried and tested (and in several countries) as few books have the opportunity to be. It is, moreover, expressly designed to fill a need specific to the present day and, beyond doubt, to the foreseeable future: a need which my experience has brought forcibly and repeatedly to my attention. This is the need to explain and show exactly *how* grammar in particular and writing in general should be learnt and taught, rather than merely *what* should be learnt and taught. More on this later in this Preface and also elsewhere in this book.

What is more, I can also safely claim that the present edition is even further improved. In the first place, I have been able to take advantage of suggestions and—whisper it!—even corrections offered by readers of the British edition who have been kind enough to contact me with them. In the second place, two chapters have been added. One of them is of considerable importance in my opinion. It is on how to compose the real verse of which genuine poetry has traditionally been held to consist. This skill, once taught to schoolchildren and necessary for even the most elementary appreciation of poetry, let alone for its composition, has been for so long abandoned as to be all but lost; and I rejoice that this book can make a contribution to restoring something that is almost unimaginably worthwhile.

When, near the beginning of this book's life in England, the time came for the second edition, there was a problem with the whole concept of a book such as this that it was well worth trying to solve. This was simply that even diligent mastery of the book's contents would still leave many readers of it somewhat up in the air as to what they could achieve in the way of good writing.

Acquiring an effortless command of grammar, although normally the indispensable foundation of writing that is competent or better, is only part of the struggle in the process of learning to write well consistently. Once that technical side is learnt, what then needs careful study is how to apply it in order to produce whatever effect one wishes to at any time. That is to say: how to make one's writing crystal-clear, or attractive and enjoyable, or persuasive, or compelling, or any or all of those. That is further to say: how to develop a writing *style* capable of suiting any useful purpose.

Like grammar, style is fundamentally a *science,* just as much a science as are any of the physical sciences to which the term is nowadays more commonly applied. Only when this science has been studied and mastered is the student in a position to develop the *individual* style that will set his or hers apart from everyone else's.

Modern "child-centred" education theory denies this, of course. For the last several decades the public has been preposterously asked to believe that methodically learning the basics of how to do something destroys a child's creativity. Common sense and thousands of years of tradition tell us, on the contrary, that the techniques of *any* activity, from composing poems to playing tennis, must be carefully learnt *as a science*—often very painstakingly in the case of the most satisfying and enjoyable occupations—before the budding practitioner can hope to flourish at it.* Providentially, there presented itself a solution to the problem of how to help users of this book acquire the *general* elements of good writing style, from which to develop the styles that their individual inherited abilities make possible, and it was a solution that seems to me as good as could reasonably be hoped for. Moreover, a remarkable feature of it is that it came from America, and yet is more suitable for this particular purpose than anything I believe to exist in England. In 1918, a professor at Cornell University, William Strunk, privately published a little book that he had written for the use of his students and others at Cornell. He called it *The Elements of Style*. Occasionally revised, it was kept in print

---

* For those many who have never been taught what everyone used to be expected to know, it may be helpful if I summarise the distinctions between science, on the one hand, and art, on the other hand, in any field:

(a) *Science* refers to knowledge. *Art,* whether in the useful or mechanical arts, on the one hand, or in the aesthetic or fine arts, on the other, refers to practice.

(b) Science tends to be based on universal laws and to be valid for everyone and for all times. Art is more personal and more changeable according to time and place. I said "*tends to be* based" rather than "*is* based" because there are exceptions. Grammar, for instance, is undoubtedly a science, but all languages change during their history and therefore their grammar to some extent with them.

(c) Science is acquired by study. Art is acquired chiefly by practice, putting into effect the science that has first been learnt.

Thus the facts and principles included in this little volume fall under the heading of science. The decisions of what to include and exclude and how to put them all together fall under the heading of art.

in a small way, until, in 1957 and after Strunk's death, one of his early students, Elwyn Brooks White, was commissioned by Macmillan publishing house to revise it so as to make it suitable for the general trade. Macmillan's judgement was vindicated indeed. To date, more than ten million copies of this extraordinary book have been sold, and it has even been the subject of a published "biography."

Some observations by E. B. White, in the book's latest edition, still in print, will do much to show why *The Elements of Style* in its original form is exactly suited to our purpose. It is extraordinarily compact. It fits, White says, the vast number of rules and principles of English on the head of a pin. It concentrates especially on the rules of usage and principles of composition most commonly violated. It aims at cleanliness, accuracy and brevity in the use of English. It does so with a vigour that has never been matched. Indeed, as White puts it, "Boldness is perhaps its chief distinguishing mark . . . He scorned the vague, the tame, the colorless, the irresolute." It is effortlessly readable.

To that, I add that all of this comes without any trace of quirkiness. On the contrary, what Professor Strunk has given to the world, in an astonishingly small space for so much, is clearly the product of painstaking study of the best authors of his time and deep and systematic thought.

At the risk of appearing extravagant, I even go so far as to estimate Strunk's little book as a minor work of genius. In respect of its many virtues, there has certainly never been anything else like it, and I can safely say that even very experienced writers can benefit from it, to increase their ability to convey their message exactly, clearly, elegantly, and in every respect in the most effective possible way. Discerning reader, whatever your present level of competence at writing English, you have much to look forward to in Part II.

"But," it may reasonably be asked, "why take up space with Strunk's relatively little-known original, when White's revised edition has been enjoying astonishing success over many decades and is readily available?"

It is with hesitation that I express reservations about one of the best-selling and presumably most influential textbooks of all time, but I believe that the original serves our purpose better than does White's revision, beautifully written and well-considered though the latter is.

One advantage of the original is its length; and its extraordinary *conciseness* was indeed something that White himself recognised as an advantage. The beauty of such compactness is that the contents can really be *learnt,* to an extent which is much more difficult, and in most cases less likely to happen, when the material is presented at significantly greater length.

After all, Strunk himself obviously *could* have made the book longer, and in a sense more complete, if he had thought that the book and its readers would benefit as a result. He chose not to, and, for someone capable of writing something as extraordinarily and memorably effective as his book is, this must surely have been for good reason. And, especially from his long experience as a teacher (which White did not have—he was not a teacher himself, but an author and journalist), Strunk must surely have been a reliable judge of such things. Indeed, we can be by no means certain that Strunk would have approved of the revised version.

Perhaps as important, White's effort gives the impression of being a much more complete treatment of the writing of English than it in fact is. This has led to the book's being widely treated as a *comprehensive* textbook on how to handle the English language, even though it is hopelessly unsuitable and inadequate for that purpose, with, for instance, nowhere in it to be found such basic elements of grammar as definitions of the sentence or of any of the parts of speech. Generation after generation, it has been widely used in schools as the only textbook for the learning of English writing. The results have been inevitably dire, since, for such a purpose, it is hopelessly unsuitable. Indeed, it should not even be *opened* until, first of all, the technical basics of writing—the elementary grammar consisting of accidence (word forms and types) and syntax (sentence construction)—have been completely mastered. This of course is exactly how Strunk has been fitted into *Gwynne's Grammar.*

One last reason to be wary of White's version of Strunk is worth mentioning, if only for the sake of completeness. Strangely, though both Strunk and White could write well, neither of them was by any means an expert on grammar. As others have noticed, both the original and the White version include extraordinary blunders where they deal with grammar, and the fact that they have never been cleaned out of the White version, even though it has been in existence for well over fifty years, has gone through several editions and has been read by literally millions of people, is surely telling. (I of course hope they have all been cleaned out here!)

In short, the fact that the original is out of copyright is by no means my only reason for preferring it for our purpose.

What is reproduced here, as Part II, is Strunk's 1918 classic, now in the public domain. I have improved the way it is set out, made a few adjustments to reflect and make clear differences between American English and British English, ventured occasional corrections, and removed a chapter which now serves no evident useful purpose.

I think it worth drawing attention to something that I have taken considerable trouble over. A rather dismaying feature of many modern books on grammar, even ones so good that I include them enthusiastically in the "Further Reading" chapter, is the inclusion of occasional errors in the grammatical information they give.

This is especially so in relation to well-known points of dispute, such as the split infinitive and the modern use of the adverb "hopefully." In such cases, of which there are relatively few, I have gone to the trouble to find out and to show what the undoubtedly correct usage is and why.

I believe this to be quite an important feature of this book. It reflects the fact that, contrary to what is often supposed, English grammar is not a haphazard collection of rules that (a) happen to have been put together over the centuries and (b) happen to exist in their present form at this point of time in our history. The rules always have a *logic* underpinning them. Even the many exceptions—of which there are perhaps more than in any other language—have an identifiable logic.

Thus, whenever I do some prescribing—which means "laying down authoritatively"—I by no means do this as an authority in my own right, which of course I am not. I do it under the authority of being a conscientious conveyor of what can be *shown* to be true. Furthermore, even under that heading I am not exercising authority as such. In any disputed matter, I expect any conclusion I offer to be considered as decisive and compelling only to the extent that the arguments with which I support it *do* support it.

In the light of all this, I hope it can be seen to be reasonable that, provided that I have exercised due care in arriving at the facts, I believe prescriptiveness to be more often justified than most modern grammarians do. I believe that I have sufficiently shown, too, that, when assessing what correct grammar is or is not, we should be influenced neither by prevailing fashion nor by present-day majority vote nor by the pronouncements of acknowledged experts—and not even if those experts are unanimous—but *only* by adequate evidence.

"Our language belongs to us all," we hear it said. I deny that it is as simple as that. I maintain, on the contrary, that, when there is a good enough reason, the traditional rule should be stated all the more uncompromisingly the more it is fading away under the pressure of prevailing fashion—perhaps even stated as one to be defended for all time, and yes, even after the battle seems irretrievably lost.

My motive is not that of wishing to dictate for the sake of wishing to do so. It is one of principle, grounded on reasoned reverence for our language.

To explain. Those who speak English today have the prodigious good fortune of having inherited from our ancestors a language which has two really spectacular features. One is that it is the most widely spoken language there has ever been. The other is that during the last four centuries, it has been, together with classical Greek and Latin, one of the three great vehicles of thought, communication, science and culture of all time.

For the ordinary person, the "man in the street," which is what I myself claim to be, two clear, common-sense duties flow from this good fortune of ours.

One of these duties is to master such a valuable possession as thoroughly as we can, in order to take the fullest possible advantage of it—both for present-day use and for learning from and enjoying the best of the past.

Of the past? As opponents of the teaching of formal grammar delight to point out, English has not remained exactly the same during the last several hundred years. Only dead languages, such as classical Greek and Latin, can do that. Anything alive must grow and change. Language is no exception.

What the same opponents almost always omit to mention, however, is that the changes during the period have been remarkably small. For instance, Shakespeare can be followed nearly as easily as if the plays and sonnets were written today. Words such as "thou" and "unto" have slipped away, and the original meaning of "nice" (primarily "fastidious") has been largely lost, and words such as "X-ray" have been introduced, and "mouse" has acquired a new meaning; but such changes are far too few to make English a different language, as it undoubtedly is compared to the original Anglo-Saxon.

Moreover, by well before the turn of the nineteenth century, two hundred years ago, the English of the day was so close to being the same as ours as to be not far from identical, other than in additions needed to reflect later events and inventions. For instance, as I write this I am looking at the best possible specimen to use for comparison: William Cobbett's *English Grammar* (originally titled *Grammar of the English Language*), first published in 1817, a best-selling book of its day and for long after, and indeed still in print today very nearly two hundred years later. In style and in the grammar it teaches, it might have been written today.

What about before Cobbett? Indeed what about before Shakespeare?

The straightforward answer to those questions is likely to be startling to most readers to the extent that they may find it difficult to believe. I shall therefore give it with the help of the single most thorough and learned treatise on all aspects of the English language in my bookshelves. Here is J. M. D. Meiklejohn, at the time Professor of the Theory, History and Practice of Education in the University of St. Andrews, on page 336 of his *English Language: Its Grammar, History, and Literature* (Alfred M. Holden, 1894):

> From the date of 1485—that is, from the beginning of the reign of Henry VII—the changes in the grammar or constitution of our language are so extremely small, that they are hardly noticeable. Any Englishman of ordinary education can read a book belonging to the latter part of the fifteenth or sixteenth century without difficulty. Since that time the grammar of our language has hardly changed at all, though we have ordered and enlarged our vocabulary, and have adopted thousands of new words.

What of the English vocabulary during that period? Professor Meiklejohn supplies a complete list of those words that have greatly changed their meaning: for instance, "animosity," which meant "high spirits"; "cunning," which innocently meant "skilled"; "hobby," which meant an "ambling nag" (still preserved in "hobby horse"); "sad," which meant "earnest"; and "thought," which meant "anxiety." I have counted them, and they total one hundred and twenty-seven. A few other words have been completely lost.

The total loss of any kind, in both grammar *and* vocabulary, is minuscule in the context of the English vocabulary as a whole. What has changed very significantly has been by way of *additions,* which of course would not affect our ability to understand our ancestors but only, hypothetically, their ability to understand us.

Moreover, up until around the early 1960s, almost all changes of any kind that did take place over the years were for the better, with new words enriching the language, and small refinements of grammar and punctuation tending in the direction of greater precision and clarity.

That is to say, our language has been both improved *and guarded* by our ancestors. Changes were admitted when they were desirable *and fought off when they were not.* We should continue to do this, I maintain, as our second common-sense duty under this heading, so that we and our contemporaries can all of us continue to speak the same precious language to each other, and to understand our forefathers.

In addition to those two reasonably obvious duties, we have a third one, in my submission: this one not on a strictly practical heading, but more under the heading of the reverence I referred to above. This is to give our ancestors the respect we owe them. We of today are—as the saying goes—standing on the shoulders of giants who themselves revered what they had received and, generation after generation, took the trouble to pass it on, intact except where improved, to the next generation.

It would be an act of ingratitude and vandalism to throw that away, and also an act of ingratitude and vandalism to *let it* be thrown away without resistance. What our ancestors did for us, we owe it to them to do for ourselves and for future generations. "Our language belongs to us all?" Not in the sense that we are free to dispose of it as we happen to see fit. Our language is something that we have the use of, but we have a duty to be responsible, even to consider ourselves trustees during our period of "occupation."

That at least is how I see it.

The conclusion I am now able to arrive at is this. Having, as I say, done the study that is necessary to reach the straightforwardly correct answers on the few contentious points, I am now prepared, on the one hand, to welcome any innovations—such as new words for new things—that are useful, and, on the other hand, to fight in order to resist any changes that are not in the direction of greater richness, clarity and precision, and are not consistent with the best features of our language, the features that have been tried and tested over a long period and not found wanting.

That last paragraph serves as an introduction to a difficulty that caused me to ponder at least as much as did anything else in this book. Throughout the history of the English language up until the last few decades, the pronoun "he," when referring to an unnamed person, has been used to include both sexes. In other words, it has been used for two purposes: to refer to a member of the male sex in particular and to a member of the human race of either sex. In Britain at least, the second use was never considered remotely inappropriate or uncomfortable—female speakers and authors used it in this general sense without hesitation or objection. (Interestingly, Strunk addressed that very point in his Chapter 5, under the heading "They," as will be seen.)

This of course has changed, the use of "he" to embrace either "he" or "she" now being held by some people to be offensive to women. The result of this has been unfortunate, to say the least. Because saying "he or she," "him or her" and "his or hers" when speaking about people generally is often disagreeably clumsy, a way of avoiding doing so has arisen which is offensive to logic and common sense and shockingly illiterate when in writing. In place of "he or she" and the rest, the words "they," "them" and "their" are now often used, even when referring to only one person, as in "Any*one* who considers this modern practice acceptable has lost their mind."

Given the weight of tradition and authority supporting the all-embracing use of "he," I could easily justify defending it prescriptively and forcefully. I should, moreover, be in good company if I did, even among recent authors. I give two examples, each from a book that I wholeheartedly recommend in "Further Reading" at the end of this book.

The up-to-date edition of *The Economist*'s authoritative *Style Guide* says in a section called "political correctness":

> Some people believe the possibility of giving offence, causing embarrassment, lowering self-esteem, reinforcing stereotypes, perpetuating prejudice, victimising, marginalising or discriminating to be more important than stating the truth, never mind the chance of doing so with any verve or panache. They are wrong . . . Your first duty is to the truth.
>
> You also have a duty to grammar. The struggle to be gender-neutral rests on a misconception about gender, a grammatical convention to make words masculine, feminine or neuter . . .
>
> If you believe it is "exclusionary" or insulting to women to use "he" in a general sense, you can rephrase some sentences in the plural . . . But some sentences resist this treatment: "Find *a* good *teacher and take his advice*" is not easily rendered gender-neutral. So do not be ashamed of sometimes using "man" to include women, or making "he" do for "she."
>
> And, so long as you are not insensitive in other ways, few women will be offended if you restrain yourself from putting "or she" after every "he."

Simon Heffer, in his *Strictly English,* published as recently as 2010, is if anything even more emphatic. His opening of the book is a Preliminary Note titled "A Word About Sex," where he says:

> We have no single pronoun to cover the phrases *he-or-she, him-or-her* and *his-or-her.* An attempt has been made in the last century or so to fill this void with *they, them* and *their.* I regard that as abominable and want no part of it . . . I adopt the old rule that "the masculine will be taken to include the feminine wherever necessary." This implies no offence to my women readers. It implies my desire to avoid the tedious verbosity of sentences such as "every writer likes to ensure that his or her command of the language . . ." So when you read "every writer likes to ensure that his command of the language . . ." please be assured that I am thinking of Jane Austen, George Eliot, Virginia Woolf and Barbara Pym as much as I am of anyone else.

I could therefore justify going to war on behalf of the traditional "he."

It is not, however, as obvious that I should do so as may at first appear. *Style Guide* and *Strictly English* are aimed principally at writers who are experts or budding experts. This book is aimed principally at beginners. So widely entrenched has the avoidance of the indeterminate "he" become by now that it may be genuinely new to some readers and possibly annoying to others.

This matters particularly in a book such as this. I do wish my readers to be able to concentrate their full attention on the information and instructions I am putting in front of them, and any distractions will result in some loss. Therefore, dear readers, I am compromising for one of only two times in this book. On the one hand, I for the most part have taken trouble to avoid using "he" to cover both sexes, though I never do what Mr. Heffer regards as abominable—for instance, using "their" when referring back to "anyone" or "no one." On the other hand, just occasionally I shall use it deliberately—I think it worth making it clear to the reader that it does exist, if only as a reminder that in finding it intolerable, he (!) would be taking a step in the direction of cutting himself off from almost the whole of English literature. Also, I have not disturbed Strunk where he does it, which is routinely.

Oh, and one other thing under this heading of modernisms. The word to indicate whether someone is male or female is "sex," not "gender," which is a purely grammatical term. "Sex" and "gender" are completely distinct words. For instance, objects of neuter *sex,* neither masculine nor feminine, can have masculine and feminine *genders.* This happens rarely in English—ships and sometimes countries are examples of where it does. In most other languages it is normal, however. Thus the neuter-sexed and neuter-gendered English "table" is the feminine-gendered *mensa* in Latin, the feminine-gendered *la table* in French, and the masculine-gendered *der Tisch* in German; and the obviously female-sexed "girl" manages to be the neuter-gendered *das Mädchen* in German.

Against the illiterate modern use of "gender," therefore, I do believe it right that I and my readers, if they can be persuaded to, should fight.

spelling

Under this general heading of conventions, I need to make specific mention of two in relation to this American edition. The first concerns spelling. After the then-inhabitants of what is now the United States of America finally succeeded in becoming independent of Britain in the eighteenth century, some scholars among them went to some trouble to reform the spelling of our common language, in order to make it better reflect how English sounds. In fact, they could never have succeeded without making American English and British English unrecognisable to each other, because the English spelling is much too far removed from how it sounds, and early attempts were obvious failures. One such scholar, however, Noah Webster, by making his modifications very few, did succeed in imposing those by means of his dictionary, which is the ultimate source of the American spelling of English today.

Nevertheless, I have kept the British-English spelling of the original edition of this book. In the first place, my keeping of the British spelling does not require *complete* defiance on my part, because, for instance, my 1928 edition of *Webster's Collegiate Dictionary* gives "practice" and "practise" as alternative spellings for the verb in question and also alternative spellings such as "color" and "colour" for British words ending in "-our." In the second place, my keeping of the British spelling is intended partly as a protest against Webster and his followers, for I maintain that Webster, in his supposed quest for a more logical spelling, in fact ended up making the spelling of English *even more* illogical than is the original spelling. For instance, American spelling favours "practice" for the verb as well as for the noun; and yet it is forced by the slightly different pronunciations of the two words to distinguish "advise" for the verb from "advice" for the noun. Similarly, while the British-English spelling of "colour" and "endeavour" were changed by Webster into "color" and "endeavor," such words as "source" and "courage" kept their spellings (why indeed not "sorse" rather than "source" to be consistent?— and, for that matter, why not "culler"?).

The other convention of which I need to make mention relates to punctuation. Under this heading, I am making my second and only other compromise in this book, and doing so in a certain amount of distress.

What is mainly at issue is the comma when it appears together with quotation marks, so that they are next to each other. A typical example of where this can happen is in a list—for instance: "His grammar was variously described as 'abysmal,' 'appalling,' 'awful,' 'horrific,' 'horrendous,' 'horrifying' and, quite simply, 'outrageous beyond belief.' "

What is open to dispute, in the punctuation of that sentence, is where the quotation marks should go in relation to the commas and the closing period. Before or after?

The standard convention in England is to put the quotation marks *before* the comma or closing period. The sentence just given as an example would therefore read: "His grammar was variously described as 'abysmal', 'appalling', 'awful', 'horrific', 'horrendous', 'horrifying' and, quite simply, 'outrageous beyond belief'."

And so—I maintain—it most certainly should. There is no logical case for putting the punctuation marks in question in any other order. In lists such as the one in the example just given, the comma is in effect replacing the conjunction "and", for the purpose of making the sentence sound better. Suppose we were to change the sentence to: "His grammar was variously described as 'abysmal' and 'appalling' and 'awful' and 'horrific'" and so on. It has of course become ungainly by comparison. In both versions, the quotation marks belong to each word individually and alone, for the purpose of isolating that word. One would certainly not say: ". . . as 'abysmal and' 'appalling and' 'awful and'" and so on. And there is no better reason for putting the quotation marks after the comma than there is for putting it, obviously insanely, after the "and to".

Thus it was throughout the English edition of this book, and I hope my trans-Atlantic readers will sympathise with me in my dismay when I saw the first printed proof of this American edition and found that, in every single such instance, the quotation marks–comma order had been reversed.

At the cost of some labour, I reversed them back again and, when returning the proof, explained why I had done so. I pointed out the clear illogicality of the American convention. I added that this illogicality was increased by another American convention under the same heading: the convention that this supposedly unimpeachable rule did not apply to semicolons, periods, question marks and exclamation marks, where, in self-contradiction, the logical order of the mother-country's practice was retained.

In other words, I only need to add a few words here and there in the example I have been using, just enough of them to justify semicolons in the place of some of the commas, to produce this remarkably punctuated sentence: "His grammar was variously described as 'abysmal'; and as often as not as 'appalling'; and even, intending no exaggeration, as 'awful'; and, even worse and scarcely less frequently, as 'horrific,' 'horrendous' and 'horrifying'; not to mention, though admittedly only once, 'outrageous beyond belief.'"

In that sentence, punctuated exactly as the authoritative *Chicago Manual of Style* prescribes, sometimes the closing quotation marks are *inside* the punctuation that follows them and sometimes they are *outside* it—specifically, four times *in front of* a semicolon and three times *after* a comma or period. In other words, in a single sentence, the sentence in question is forced to contradict itself logically several times. To descend, in my exasperation, into the vernacular for the first of only two times in this book: the convention I was being asked to adopt is bonkers.

My gracious publisher admitted some embarrassment as he begged me not to insist on the English practice that I had laboured to restore. Keeping the original punctuation, he said, far from having any useful effect in, for instance, launching a crusade against punctuation-madness, would lead potential readers only to question, or more than question, the value of the book even as a guide to grammar, and all too probably to end up dismissing it out of hand. And at least, he added, the American convention was consistent, in the sense that it was universally used in America, with all the style guides, led by the aforesaid *Chicago Manual*, in agreement in prescribing this crazy—my word, not his—convention.

Perhaps I should hang my head in shame, dear reader, but I caved in. Although it is far from being my view that a majority vote or even a unanimous one can ever legitimately decide what is true and reasonable, my larger aims would hardly be served if, by reason of my uncompromising firmness in this matter, I smothered the very discussion I meant to spark about grammar. Therefore, I am confining my objections to these few paragraphs in this Preface. Who knows? Perhaps they will suffice to launch a crusade of their own, one that shall overturn all reigning American authority in punctuation, finally obliging my publisher to issue a new edition.

I turn to an interesting feature that I claim to be a considerable merit of this book. This is in fact an *absence* of a feature that has come to be expected in any textbook on any subject. I believe it worth drawing attention to if only because it will occur to very few readers that it is an advantage if I do not.

The following pages are free from the pointless and patronising pictures that have been the bane of almost every textbook on every single academic subject during the last fifty years and more. Where pictures belong is for illustrating what cannot adequately be taught without them, nowhere else—and nowhere else were they ever included in traditional textbooks. Examples of pictures that are needed are maps in geography textbooks and illustrations of skeletons of animals in biology textbooks.

Please do not think that this is a neutral matter and that the only advantage of doing without pictures is that of saving space. Pictures in textbooks actually interfere with the learning process, and not long ago I was given a useful example of this damage definitely occurring in practice. Two parents in America, both of them academically highly qualified, had a four-year-old son who was showing every sign of having inherited their intelligence. He was already such a voracious reader that he kept a different book in every room in their house so that, wherever he was, he could pick up one of his books and continue reading it. Essential to his constant desire to read was that the books should have no pictures. If any book did have pictures, he simply did not read it but looked at the pictures instead.

Thus he would not have learnt—or at least would not have learnt from self-motivation—to read at his age even from, for instance, the best-selling Ladybird books in Britain, which first really got going in the 1960s and have pictures on every alternate page, let alone from the more modern books for children that often have more pictures than text.

I have some closing words addressed directly to you, dear reader.

Unless you are already well acquainted with the material that is in this book, I can safely say that you will emerge from it a different person from the person that you are now—and for the better—and all the more so, the more effort you put into mastering what is to be found in it. In saying this, I am not making any claims on my own behalf. Even though my experience makes it clear that most of what is in this book will be new to most of its readers, there is, in fact, virtually nothing original in it except its manner of presentation. I am referring only to the effect that improvement in grammar must unfailingly have on both mind and character.

As we grow in both the extent and the exactness of our knowledge of the language which enables, governs, and even limits our ability to think, our minds become sharper and clearer, our characters become more independent and confident, and our ability to appreciate and make the best of what we are surrounded with is enriched.

And even if we consider the negative aspect alone of what we are doing, no one ever, ever, ever would have preferred to know less grammar than he does know.

There is more on the value of grammar in Chapters 2 and 3. Meanwhile, I hope I have succeeded in encouraging you to turn to Chapter 1 in an eager frame of mind.

—N. M. GWYNNE

nmgwynne@eircom.net

www.gwynneteaching.com

23rd June 2014

PART I

Gwynne's Grammar

CHAPTER 1

This Is a Serious Business

Let no one be deceived into thinking that learning grammar is a luxury of relatively little importance, on the basis of such specious reasoning as that most people today manage to communicate adequately without having ever studied it formally. Learning even one's own language without systematically learning its grammar is far slower and less efficient than otherwise. And anyway, even the most intelligent people seldom *do* get a completely accurate grasp of English from a grammarless education and can all too easily make elementary mistakes—such as "Between you and I" and the politically correct illiteracy "Any*one* in doubt should ask *their* teacher"—that would never have been made at any level of society fifty or sixty years ago.

It is as well to emphasise that *effortless* knowledge of

these elementary basics of grammar is indispensable for accurate English, Latin and Greek, and any other European language. In what follows, at least the definitions **in bold print** should be learnt *exactly* by heart, including even their word order. All the other definitions and explanations should at least be thoroughly *understood,* and learners should be able easily to think up sentences of their own that give examples of any of the defined terms.

The other use of bold print is to indicate the first time any important term is used in any discussion of it to make it easier to find it whenever you need to.

CHAPTER 2

A Note of Encouragement

Here is a step-by-step proof (yes, a proof that really *is* valid!) that happiness depends partly on grammar.

Step one. For genuine thinking, we need words. (By "genuine thinking" I mean as opposed to merely being conscious of feeling hungry, tired, angry and so on and wanting to do something about it; in other words, anything that animals cannot do.) Thinking cannot be done without words.

Step two. If we do not use words rightly, we shall not think rightly.

Step three. If we do not think rightly, we cannot reliably decide rightly, because good decisions depend on accurate thinking.

Step four. If we do not decide rightly, we shall make a

mess of our lives and also of other people's lives to the extent that we have an influence on other people.

Step five. If we make a mess of our lives, we shall make ourselves and other people unhappy.

In summary of the proof: grammar is the science of using words rightly, leading to thinking rightly, leading to deciding rightly, without which—as both common sense and experience show—happiness is impossible. *Therefore,* happiness depends at least partly on good grammar.

Nor does the importance of grammar stop there. Let us expand on some of the elements of the proof just given and also take the proof a little further.

Step one. Words are what we think with as well as communicate with. Without words, we can *feel* (tired, hungry, angry and so on), but we cannot *think.* We cannot *reason things out,* not even the simplest things.

Step two. From *Step one* it then follows that if we are to *think* correctly and usefully, words need to be *used* correctly, obviously.

Step three. Using words correctly involves two sciences. One of them is *vocabulary,* the science of what words *mean.* The other is *grammar,* the science of *how* words are used in order to *have* thoughts and to *convey* thoughts—in the form of either statements, questions, wishes or commands. Although vocabulary is in one sense the primary science of all sciences, because we cannot have grammar without words to be grammatical with, it is also the case that vocabulary depends, practically speaking, on grammar. We even need grammar in order to understand vocabulary—to understand the definitions in a dictionary.

Step four. Vocabulary and grammar—words and the correct use of words—are therefore the sciences that are the *necessary* prelude to the science of thinking. The science of thinking is technically known as *logic.*

Step five. Logic, in turn, is the *necessary* prelude to the science of communicating, which includes arguing and debating (which in turn include how to spot and see through attempts to bamboozle us with bogus arguments), and is technically known as the science of *rhetoric.*

Step six. On these four sciences—vocabulary, grammar, logic, and rhetoric—*all other sciences,* without exception, depend.

Step seven. We turn now to the taking of decisions. Even at the simplest level, that of taking decisions big or small, the quality of our decisions is going to depend on the accuracy and clarity of the thinking we put into them, and bad decisions adversely affect our well-being, our happiness and the happiness of people who are affected by us.

Step eight. It does not stop there. If enough people in any society are incompetent in their thinking and in consequence take bad decisions, their bad decisions inevitably affect the whole of that society. The very well-being of society therefore depends in part on good grammar.

Step nine. Would that the harmful effects of bad grammar stopped there. They do not. *Civilisation itself* exists only in the various societies that make it up. If enough societies in the world crumble as a result of bad decisions taken because of bad thinking, yes, the whole of world civilisation faces collapse, with consequences for each individual that are literally incalculable.

As an argument for the usefulness of this little book, all of that is dramatic and far-reaching indeed. And the logic supporting the case is sufficiently clear-cut to be its own authority. After all, what is demonstrably true is true even if no one believes it. Truth is not decided by majority vote, nor even by unanimous vote, nor even by the majority or unanimous vote of experts.

Even so, given that those most influential in education during the last few decades have been completely dismissive of grammar, some readers may at least be comforted to know that far from my being in isolation in stressing the unique importance of grammar, others clearly well placed to make a judgement have recently seen fit to air the same view in even stronger language than I have been using.

Libby Purves, experienced broadcaster, journalist and author, OBE for services to journalism, and 1999 Columnist of the Year, in an article in *The Times* of London on 27 August 2012 wrote:

Of all school disciplines English language matters most. Clarity, confidence, communication are the bedrock of every other endeavour in education and in life: from physics to marketing, from engineering to law. Neglecting, downgrading and generally dumbing standards is a greater cruelty to children than anything visited on them by a clumsy exam board . . . It is wicked not to emphasise the difference between chatty street slang and formal, universally understood, clarity and correctness.

Dot Wordsworth, long-serving columnist for the weekly *Spectator,* also used the word "cruel" in an article in the *Daily Telegraph* of 6 July 2012:

It's cruel not to teach children grammar . . . Pupils (or students as they are mysteriously called) are not taught such rules of spelling as may exist and certainly are not tested on them. As for adverbs, subjects, objects or clauses, let alone such fabulous monsters as subjunctives, children are left in sublime ignorance of them . . . At its worst, educational theory that rejects grammar does so because of a mad idea that children are noble savages better left to authenticity and the composition of rap lyrics. That way lies the scrapheap and jail. Grammar sets them free. No one would think it a kindness to give a teenager a car without teaching her[*] to drive, and that includes the rules of the road.

The word "cruel" is perhaps especially appropriate and telling, given that it is quite commonly used against those who hold that grammar should be imposed on children for their lasting benefit.

Cruel? *Every* worthwhile skill needs effort to acquire it, and even some of the purely enjoyable ones need very considerable effort. Does anyone ever look back and regret the effort made? On the contrary, no one who reaches a level of skill in *any* field *ever* wishes that he had a lower degree of skill in that field. In whatever you undertake, you want to reach, within reason, as high a standard in that field as your inborn capabilities make possible. All the more is this so with grammar, when *everything* depends on it.

Ergo: whether with reference to saving civilisation, at one extreme, or to protecting from appalling cruelty a single little child over whom you have some influence, at the other extreme, the importance of grammar as the primary step in any education is actually beyond the possibility of exaggeration.

---

* Note the "her"! N.M.G.

CHAPTER 3

Further Encouragement

Against the background of the last chapter, I find myself provoked into raising a question of some moment. Have I your attention, dear reader? Here is the question.

Is this book that you have in your hands, in a way that really does matter, the single most important book in print in the English language today?

At most, I am only partly joking. What I am trying to do is to make a serious point as arrestingly and vividly as I can. I certainly deny that what I have just said is completely absurd. Let us now see if it is at least defensible.

As has just been shown, and as was stressed by Libby Purves in the previous chapter, all thinking and communicating of any kind depend on grammar—grammar being simply the correct use of words, and words being the indispensable tools of thought.

Indeed to dismiss the need for the accuracy in grammar that only reasonably diligent study and training can give is almost self-contradictory. You need correct grammar even to be able to argue as convincingly as you can against the need to learn grammar.

To proceed. If every human activity depends ultimately on language, all that is left, in order to assess my claim, is to weigh up whether or not this book does the particular job it sets out to do better than any other book on grammar in print today.

There is one significant difference between this book and any of its predecessors and contemporaries, and indeed between this book and any other book setting out to teach *any* academic subject. This book does not only teach what must be taught. It also tries to teach *how best* to teach what must be taught, for the purpose of making sure that the learner will absorb, understand and remember what he or she is trying to learn.

I have listed those aims—absorb, understand and remember—in that order, because it is their order of importance. The order of *teaching* those three elements should be the opposite. Contrary to education theory most widely propagated today, memorising should come first, preferably starting before understanding is even possible—that is, before what is commonly called the age of reason, about seven. The period before the age of reason happens to be the age when memorising is easiest. It is also the age when the vital task of memory training is most effectively done.

This very much applies to some of the material in this book, which, as stated in Chapter 1, needs to be learnt *by heart* for it to be most useful, or indeed in some cases for it to be of any use at all. I know this from the many pupils of all ages that I have been teaching in recent years. Merely to *understand* a rule is almost never sufficient. Unless it is *memorised,* and in such a way as to *keep* it in the memory, all too soon, typically, children are as incapable of applying the rule as if they had never come across it.

I can "hear" protests. "It is not treating children with the dignity they deserve to stuff their memories with what they cannot understand."

Do not believe it.

First, no such objection is made to children's learning the genuinely incomprehensible "Eeny, meeny, miny, mo."

Secondly, I repeat that the period before they reach the age of reason, at about seven years old, is when children find learning by heart easiest of all; and we are hardly being cruel by spending part of that time giving them a bank of knowledge which is ready and waiting to be used as soon as they become capable of using it and giving their memories valuable training at the same time.

Thirdly, contrary to what is often supposed, children typically relish doing it. If you doubt me, you might like to visit the Gwynne Teaching Web site. There you will see some of my youngest pupils reciting—sometimes for considerable periods of time—things they do not yet understand, such as multiplication tables and Latin nouns and verbs, often beaming enthusiastically as they do so.

If I have made something of a case in answer to the question at the beginning of this chapter, my main purpose has been less to boast, you my readers may be comforted to learn, than to stress yet further the supreme importance—supreme *practical* importance—of what you and I are engaged in together as you go through this book. My aim in doing so is to persuade you to be prepared to take on the genuinely hard work of tackling the science of your language, whether you be pupil or teacher. Just *reading* this book will achieve relatively little, however enlightening and helpful you may find what you read. What is in this book must be *mastered*. How best to set about doing this will be discussed in Chapter 9.

CHAPTER 4

Does Prescriptiveness *Really* Belong to Grammar?

As readers with retentive memories will remember, I opened the subject of prescriptiveness in the Preface. It is worth looking at the subject further, because it is one that is so much at the heart of what this book is for.

As must by now be obvious, it is my position that the prescriptive approach to grammar, the one that says some things are right and some things are wrong, rather than merely describing things as they are, is the only correct approach. In this, I am not being original; until recently, it was always so assumed. Practically, what it means is that grammar involves rules, which in turn means that learning grammar involves *learning* rules, which in yet another turn means learning what the rules are, how to obey them, and finally how to master them. Such mastery can only be achieved by painstaking care and much practice, preferably under competent instruction if such be available.

What kind of rules are these? They fall into three categories.

The first consists of rules that are absolute and can never be broken. For example, the sentence "Between you and *I,* we are being taught by *she,* to *who* I am very grateful" includes three errors, each of which can never be acceptable and must always be proscribed.

The second consists of rules that are generally valid but can be broken judiciously for special effect. A condition of doing so is that it be done only rarely. Otherwise, in the first place, the discriminating reader can see that the purpose is insufficient to justify the breach; and, in the second place, the "specialness" of the effect is by very definition diluted by the usage being, *not* special, but commonplace. Under this heading, an example is the use of conjunctions such as "And," "But," "Or" and "So" as first words in sentences. Because this rule allows some flexibility, how it is practised can vary from era to era.

The third does not belong to formal writing, but only to colloquial speaking and to "light-hearted" writing. It consists of breaking some of the rules normally to be considered as absolute, though by no means all or even most of them, but breaking them so flagrantly that the reader can tell that the writer knows what he is up to. When, for instance, Churchill wished to make a point about the rule that a sentence should never end with a preposition, he is said to have written, "Ending a sentence with a preposition is something up with which I shall not put."

Now, one might ask, why should rules be needed at all? Why is it not sufficient, as many today would claim, to express one's thoughts as one sees fit, and without being restricted and hampered in how one does it?

To put that question to the majority of those in, and influential over, the teaching profession today would be to invite a snorted: "Quite so. Your question is self-answering." Furthermore, such authorities could well insist, to spend the time and effort involved in following rules is not merely pointless, as it obviously is, given that English is a living language and therefore constantly changing, as living languages always are. In addition, it takes up time that would be better spent by the student on being creative, and, being highly off-putting, it may even retard development. What a child needs to cultivate is a *love* of writing, and insisting on rules that must be complied with can only be destructive of that end.

Subject closed? "By no means," answers tradition stretching back literally thousands of years. However burdensome mastering rules may be—and that burden varies from person to person—so be it. Acquiring new skills of any worth is always going to be burdensome. *Using* those skills once mastered, however, is not. On the contrary, handling our language properly is satisfying, enjoyable, a source of confidence, and even in a sense comforting, just as is being "on top of" *any* activity that one wishes to engage in. It does involve taking trouble, which for instance often includes much redrafting of prose by even the best authors. This book does not aim at saving you trouble, however, other than unnecessary trouble. Rather it aims at helping you to create something that will do the job that you want it to do, that you can rejoice over, and that will always be a credit to you. The only difference in this respect between producing good English and any other worthwhile activity is that the former is the most important activity of all, and the one most worth taking trouble over.

Nowadays, if grammar is taught at all, which is much more in books—a remarkable quantity of which has been published in recent years—than in schools, the grammar in question is said to be based on what is generally regarded as best *today* but ever changing and likely to be different tomorrow. Even most authors on the subject today would scarcely, if ever, deny that, and most expressly support it. Nevertheless, as so often with what I find myself needing to say in this book, this view is very much a minority one in the history of the English language dating back well over a thousand years. It is as well, therefore, to have a quick look at some highlights of the history of English grammar and the teaching of it, to the extent that it is relevant in this context.

As mentioned in the Preface, English grammar has not changed in any essentials since before the turn of the sixteenth century; in other words, not for more than five hundred years. Vocabulary has changed, though much less so than is often claimed in today's scholarship on the subject, and punctuation too to a modest extent, in the direction of refinement of it. Grammar basically has not.

What *has* changed is how grammar has been learnt. Read, for instance, a piece of prose written in the early 1700s by the famous essayist Joseph Addison. You will find that with very few exceptions such as nouns starting with capital letters (as still happens in German), and "ask'd" and "answer'd" rather than their modern equivalents, it might almost have been written today.

At schools, all the leading ones of which were called *grammar* schools, English grammar was not taught as a separate subject. For any normal purpose for which writing was needed, from the composition of a scientific treatise to keeping household accounts, Latin was the language used, and Latin grammar was what was taught, with English grammar being picked up as a "side-effect" of that. This indeed was still how English was being taught when I was at school. We did not have English-language teachers as such; we learnt it as part of our training in the classical languages.

This is not to suggest that English grammar comes anywhere near to being the same as Latin grammar. In fact, the two grammars could hardly be more unalike. The grammar terminology is the same, however, adopted from Latin, and the very difference between the two languages forced one to be punctiliously attentive to the most minute details of English grammar in order to translate satisfactorily in either direction.

What contributed most of all to bringing about change in the attitude to English was its starting to replace Latin as the language in which serious scientific works were written, in the seventeenth century. With these, and indeed on any subject needing to be closely argued, it mattered that even the slightest shade of meaning be completely clear, as was quickly recognised. The first English dictionaries and books on English grammar started appearing then, and those that received general approval were used as authorities—not as mere *records* of usage, but as *prescribers* of it. They have poured out ever since and, whenever they were written, were always in substantial agreement with each other until recently as to what is *correct,* rather than anything resembling current fashion.

So it is that a book on my shelves written in the eighteenth century, *The Rudiments of English Grammar, Adapted to the Use of Schools* by Joseph Priestley, would, with very little alteration, serve very adequately as a book for use in schools today, as would many of its predecessors dating some time back. Always, though, they were used against the background of Latin's being the primary subject taught at schools.

Nowadays, and as of the last fifty years, Latin is largely excluded as a subject taught in schools, and even where it still exists or has been brought back, it is almost never taught as it used to be taught, starting with the systematic and intensive learning of grammar of the language. Simultaneously, far from English grammar's being more thoroughly taught in order to compensate for that, it too has been abolished almost everywhere, supposedly from, as already mentioned, fear of stifling the expressive creativity of children, and, no less shockingly, because of the notion that there can be no wrong way to use the language.

It is a serious matter, and, even though more people are waking up to the reality than ever before in the last fifty years, it is becoming more serious all the time. Until recently, children were taught to regard writing as something over which they needed to take much trouble, including seeking to imitate the best writers of the past. As of the last two decades, the effects of computers having largely replaced writing by hand, of the influence of the Internet, and of the emergence of texting have been to engulf us in a tidal wave of writing the first thing that comes into our heads in the quickest possible way, and irrespective of quality in how we express ourselves.

Indeed, texting is creating a language of its own. This would matter little if "text-speak" were used only for that purpose, but it is beginning to influence how people speak and think. The reality is that it is no longer the English language that is our constant, as it has been for centuries. Now it is *change* continually going on in our language that is a constant, with communication with others of the same generation heading more and more in the direction of breaking down, at least to some extent and to an increasing extent if present trends continue. Communication with our ancestors now dead and with our successors not yet living is foreseeably becoming impossible for any serious practical purposes—something that has never happened before in all recorded history.

Against all this background, right-thinking people should surely oppose this as firmly as is within their power, rather than go along with it. Is not this book, therefore, overwhelmingly justified in emphatically prescribing prescriptiveness?

CHAPTER 5

Still Introductory

1. Grammar has two main divisions.

One of these divisions is called morphology, sometimes otherwise called accidence. Morphology deals with how words are formed and especially with how words change their form—most often their endings—when they are used for different purposes.

Examples of words changing their form—usually, but by no means always, their endings—are:

Nouns—for instance, "cat" and "cats"; "woman" and "women"; "mouse" and "mice."

Pronouns—for instance, "we" and "us"; "who," "whom" and "whose"; "this" and "these."

Adjectives—for instance, "nice," "nicer," "nicest"; and "good," "better," "best."

Verbs—for instance, "love," "loves," "loved," "loving"

(and even "lovable," though that is a pure adjective rather than any part of a verb); and "sing," "sings," "sang," "sung" and "singing"; "eat," "eats," "ate," "eaten" and "eating." Most spectacular of all, in its number of changes, is the verb "to be," which can change to "am," "is," "are," "was," "were," "been" and "being"—eight widely differing forms in total.

More on this aspect of nouns, pronouns, adjectives and verbs in Chapter 6.

The other main division of grammar is called syntax. Syntax deals with the *use* made of words, especially when words are used in combination. This usually involves (a) arranging words into *sentences* (see Chapter 7) that *represent correctly* and *express exactly* the thought of the speaker or writer, and (b) choosing the right word form for any particular purpose, as in "Have parents whose children's work has continually needed improvement ever been known to consider *better* stimuli in such crises?"

2. Because of the importance of definitions in the study of language, it is as well to know exactly what a definition is. A *definition* is a statement of the precise nature of something or the precise meaning of a word or phrase. Specifically in vocabulary and grammar, a definition is a statement of the exact meaning of a word or phrase that sufficiently distinguishes it from any other word or phrase, preferably in the fewest possible words.

The best way, indeed almost always the *right* way, to

produce the most accurate, crisp and succinct definition of anything is to divide the definition into two parts:

[handwritten margin note: Definitions]

a. the *general* group or class to which the object being defined belongs, or, in more technical terminology, the genus immediately *above* the object being defined; and

b. enough difference or differences between the object being defined and anything else in the same group, the group "above" it, to leave it standing on its own.

Both (a) and (b) must also be defined if necessary, and so on, until it is completely clear what every term in a definition means.

Thus the classic definition of a human being, "a rational animal," perfectly follows this principle, because

[handwritten note: more precise, to use "mammal"?]

a. The word "animal" embraces all beings that move, feed themselves, reproduce, feel, desire and even in some degree imagine.

b. The additional and exclusive ability of human beings to analyse and arrive at reasoned conclusions indicated by the word "rational" sufficiently distinguishes them from all other animals.

Most of the definitions in these pages follow this pattern.

The importance of definitions for *all* intellectual purposes can hardly be overestimated. "Define your terms" should be, at least implicitly, the starting point of any discussion or debate that is at all important and complicated. In the absence of clearly stated and agreed definitions, all too often two parties discussing or arguing about something will in fact either

- be discussing or arguing about different things, or
- be using arguments that are bound to be completely misunderstood, or
- both.

That said, it is notable that in grammar satisfactory definitions are sometimes difficult to come up with, other than at a length which would make them too unwieldy for students of grammar to learn from. On the face of it, this is a serious matter, given that grammar is the most important of all sciences, with every other science without exception depending on the abilities to think and communicate, and therefore on strict accuracy in the use of words.

The problem needs to be mentioned for the sake of good order, especially after so much emphasis has been put on the importance of definitions. No *practical* problems arise, however. Sometimes, as in every grammar book, we shall have to "make do" with definitions that will "do" for *practical* purposes, even though strictly speaking they are not genuine definitions. I shall always make it clear when a definition is not strictly accurate, but this will only be because I ought to as a matter of principle. An important function of this book, after all, is the promotion of exactness of the highest degree in thinking and communicating, and anyway the difficulties with definitions are often interesting. It will *not* be found that any lack of—may I say it?—definitiveness in any of the definitions will interfere with mastering the grammar that depends on them.

3. Less important than definitions, but certainly helpful and often interesting, is what is called etymology. This is the science of how words come to be as they are. Knowing how words came into the English language can often give a clearer understanding of their meaning, even when the meaning is by no means the same as it originally was, as is often the case.

In the following chapters, my aim will be to give enough derivations to show that derivations are worthy of study, rather than to be comprehensive—which is surely unnecessary bearing in mind that any good dictionary can be used to fill in any gaps. I very much hope that readers will find themselves encouraged to take an interest in the subject, however. As can scarcely be said too often, the more thoroughly and intimately we know our language, the better it is for us in every imaginable way.

Thus it is not *merely* an advantage to know why such words as "noun," "adjective" and "clause" have come to have their meanings. To take an interest in etymology is in some degree to take an interest in history. Every word is a word which came into existence at some point in time for some reason, often to fulfil a need since without it we should be unable to have the thought that it expresses.

Furthermore, the study could also open up or deepen our appreciation of the achievements in this field of our ancestors, and even motivate us to defend their achievements. Some of the words which we shall be coming across stand out as wonderfully well chosen, and are even sometimes concocted with remarkable subtlety, and at some point someone must have put together a particular word, and enough others must have recognised its value for it to become generally adopted.

That, clearly, is how language *ought* to be changed: by the adoption of words and expressions which do a job that had not been done before. Other than when used informally, as in slang, language should *not* be changed for no better reason than for some possibly amusing fashion. It should *not* be changed in any direction that makes it less precise or otherwise weaker. If etymology helps us to appreciate the cultural skills of our ancestors, we shall be less likely to commit the crime of cultural vandalism involved in letting go or damaging what we have received and more likely to want to defend it.

Thus some of the value of etymology, both in the context of what we are studying and trying to master in these pages and also in general. And since it may be helpful to illustrate what I have just been saying, let us make an immediate start by looking at the etymology of three important words in this very chapter.

Morphology is made up of two Greek words. The first of them, *morphe,* means, primarily, "shape" or "form." The second, *logos,* is possibly the single most profound word in any language. Its primary meaning is "word" in the sense of the word by which an inward thought is expressed, and its secondary meaning is the "inward thought" itself, or "reason." It also has a large number of meanings related to "word" and "reason." It is even used in the first verse of the fourth Gospel to represent the Founder of Christianity before He became incarnate—"In the beginning was the Word."

In the word "morphology," *logos* is probably best translated as "study" or "science." Combining *morphe* and *logos,* therefore, we can arrive at "The study of how individual words change their shape as we put them to different uses."

Does not that information about a word make the word more real?—and even make it easier to remember? Already I hope it is evident that etymology has a *practical* value as well as being educational in other ways.

Syntax comes from the Greek words *sun,* meaning "together with" or "along with," and *taxis,* meaning primarily "a drawing up in order of an army." From that military terminology, we get the figurative "Putting words collected together into the right order so as to make sense." Even dry-as-dust grammatical terms can be colourful in their origins.

Will you now admit, dear discerning reader, that etymology can be helpful, and not only helpful but interesting too, and not only helpful and interesting but sometimes even fun?

And the word etymology itself? *Etumos* means "true" or "real" or "actual." Etymology is therefore the study of what words *really* are, which of course is to be found in their origins.

Finally, here is an important word which we have not used before: parse. Coming, through French, from the Latin *partes,* which means "parts," parsing is analysing everything that can be analysed in a sentence into its grammatical components. Learning to parse and making the best use of the skill is much of what this book is about.

CHAPTER 6

Parts of Speech

There are eight *parts of speech:* noun, pronoun, adjective, verb, adverb, conjunction, preposition and interjection.

1. Nouns

A *noun* is the name of a person, place or thing; that is to say, it is the name of whatever we can think about. It is also sometimes called a substantive. The word comes from the Latin for "name," *nomen,* from which we also get "nominal" and "denominate."

As to names of *persons* or *places:*

a. Most nouns are common nouns. A common noun indicates a *class* of persons, places or things.

Examples of common nouns are the words "person," "place" and "thing" themselves.

b. Some nouns indicating persons and things are proper nouns. A proper noun refers to an *individual* person or place and almost always starts with a capital letter—for instance, "Socrates" and "Nile."

c. When a noun is the name of a *thing,* the thing can be:

   i. A concrete thing. A concrete thing is something which exists in a *material* form and which we can therefore see, hear, touch, taste or smell.

   ii. An abstract thing. An abstract thing is something that we can *not* perceive with our senses, because it is separate from matter. Examples are duty, goodness, sight, happiness, logic, history, circumstance and, yes, grammar.

d. Collective nouns are another important category of nouns. Examples are "crowd," "flock" and indeed "collection." According to their sense in particular cases, the same collective nouns can:

   i. sometimes be plural, as in the sentence "The audience *were* in disagreement among themselves"; and

   ii. sometimes be singular, as in "The audience *was* full of intelligent people."

     The word "jury" can of course be used in exactly the same way.

2. Pronouns

A *pronoun* is a word which stands in place of a noun. It is used to avoid clumsy, sometimes very clumsy, repetition. The word comes from the Latin *pro,* meaning "for" or "on behalf of," and of course *nomen* again.

There are various kinds of pronouns. The most basic pronouns are:

Personal pronouns. They include "I," "me," "you," "thou," "thee," "he," "him," "she," "her," "it," "we," "us," "you," "they" and "them."

Other kinds of pronouns are:

Intensive pronouns, as in "I *myself* can see it."

Reflexive pronouns, as in "I myself can see *myself.*"

Relative pronouns, such as "who," "which" and "that," as in "He *who* dares" and "The thing *that* he dares to do." Relative pronouns also join clauses together, as in "We have found the house *that* you were looking for"; and for this reason they are sometimes called *conjunctive pronouns.*

Demonstrative pronouns, such as "this" and "that," as in the famous—and ridiculous—statement "To be or not to be: *that* is the question."

Demonstrative adjectives. These are not in fact pronouns but adjectives and will be dealt with under that heading. I am making reference to them here simply because the words used as demonstrative pronouns are also used as adjectives, as in "*this* or *that* question."

Interrogative pronouns, such as "who," "whoever,"

[handwritten marginalia: "?" and "restrictive pronouns or unrestrictive"]

"which" and "what," this time starting questions, as in "*Who* dares?," "*Whoever* can it have been that made that noise?," "*Which* of you made that noise?" and "*What* is the time?"

Indefinite pronouns, as in "*None* of us can see either *anyone* or *anything* of any importance" and "I can see *someone* and *something* of some importance."

Possessive pronouns—"mine," "yours," "thine," "his," "hers," "ours," "yours" (this time for more than one person), "theirs," as in "Yes, this book is *yours.*"

Possessive adjectives, as they are called—"my," "your," "thy," "his," "her," "its," "our," "your" again and "their." These always stand either:

a. before the noun(s) they apply to (as in "*your* grammar lessons"); or
b. before any adjective(s) immediately before the noun(s) they apply to (as in "*your* valuable grammar lessons"); or
c. before any adverb(s) immediately before any adjective(s) immediately before the noun(s) they apply to (as in "*your* wonderfully valuable grammar lessons").

It is time to point out that the definition of "pronoun," although adequate for practical purposes, is not a true definition. For instance:

If I wish to say that my pupils are making excellent pro-gress, I can substitute the word "they" for "pupils" if I have already mentioned them in the previous sentence and my new sentence is referring to exactly the same pupils. Using the pronoun "they" allows me to avoid the clumsiness of using the same noun in two successive sentences. If, however, I wish to say that "I am happy with their progress," the word "I" is simply not a true substitute for "their teacher" or me by my name. "I am . . ." and "Their teacher is . . ." are not identical. "I" therefore does not truly stand in place of any noun. Perhaps to make the point clearer, "I" is the universal pronoun for the person speaking and cannot be said to stand in place of his mere name. The same applies to "you."

"Someone" and "something" and "no one" and "nothing" do not stand in place of any nouns.

It would in fact be impossible to come up with a definition that was concise enough to be of practical usefulness. Nor, in practice, does it matter that we cannot.

3. Adjectives

An *adjective* is a word which describes a noun or a pronoun. Rather exotically, the word "adjective" comes from the past participle of the Latin word *adicio,* which breaks down into *ad,* meaning "towards" or "at," and, when it is by itself without a prefix in front of it, *iacio,* meaning "I throw." Thus, literally, an adjective is a word "thrown at" a noun; less literally, "added to" it. (What a past participle is will be found under the heading of the next part of speech, **Verbs**.)

Adjectives have also been usefully described as "the clothing" of nouns and pronouns.

There are five kinds of adjectives:

Adjectives of quality, which answer the question "Of what sort?," as in "black and white" and "good and bad."

Adjectives of quantity, which answer the question "How much?," as in "any," "few," "much," and "enough."

Adjectives of number, which answer the question "How many?," as in "one" and all the way up.

Demonstrative adjectives, which answer the question "Which?"—these have already been examined under the different heading of pronouns.

Possessive adjectives. These have already been dealt with under the heading of Pronouns.

The basic adjectives, which are called positive adjectives, can have comparatives and superlatives, both of which indicate *degrees* of the adjective in question.

A *comparative* adjective is the form of the positive adjective which makes it mean *more* of the adjective in question.

A *superlative* adjective is the form of the positive adjective which makes it mean *most* of the adjective in question. (In Latin and Greek, but not in formal English, the superlative of an adjective can also mean "very." I say "not in *formal* English" because in purely conversational English the use of the superlative to mean "very" is normal enough scarcely to fall under the heading of slang—for instance, "This book is most helpful to me, it was most kind of you to bring it to my attention, and I am most grateful.")

Examples of the *positives, comparatives* and *superlatives* of adjectives: "nice, nicer, nicest"; "good, better, best"; and "grammatical, more grammatical and most grammatical."

Note that "unique" (meaning "the only one of its kind"), "peerless," "matchless" (both of which mean "without equal"), "infinite" and "eternal" cannot have comparatives or superlatives. This is because someone or something either *is* or *is not* unique, peerless, matchless, infinite and/or eternal, and nothing can be more so. Other adjectives which, strictly speaking, cannot have comparatives or superlatives include "dead," "circular" and "brownish."

This rule dictating that certain adjectives have no superlatives *can* be broken when speaking colloquially and obviously jokily, as in "even deader than a doornail." In the case of "unique," "peerless" and others, however, to attribute any degree would always be considered, by someone competent in English, to be a mistake that had been made because of ignorance rather than deliberately as a joke.

Finally on adjectives, the order in which they are put when there is more than one describing a noun or pronoun is important. Almost always, the order is opinion, size, age, shape, colour, origin, material, purpose. The book you are holding is therefore a nice little just-published oblong-shaped attractively coloured much-needed hardcover grammar textbook. Put those adjectives in the wrong order and the meaning breaks down, which is doubtless why most people soon pick up the right order of adjectives without having to give it more than minimal thought.

Note: the *article,* consisting solely of "the," "a," "an" and "some," is sometimes reckoned as a separate part of speech. In reality, it is a kind of adjective, indeed a kind of demonstrative adjective.

4. Verbs

A *verb* is a doing or being word. The same definition can be alternatively worded as a *verb* is a word which expresses an action or a state. The word "verb" comes from the Latin word *verbum,* meaning "word." The reason for this name is that a verb is *the* word in any sentence—leave it out and all the other words cease to make sense. A good definition for young beginners is simply "a telling word."

The doing, as opposed to being, kind of verb can be either transitive or intransitive. What these terms mean is given and explained on page 69, but they are mentioned here because the term "transitive" needs to be used later in this chapter.

Verbs are much, much the most complex parts of speech to describe.

4.1. Tenses. Arguably, the most important division of verbs is into *tenses,* which show *when* the action is *being done* (or might be done, or should be done, and so on) or *when* the state is *in being*—that is to say, either in the *present here and now* or in the *future* or in the *past.* Tenses which do *basically* the same jobs often have different names and slightly different functions (that is, do slightly different jobs) in different languages. For instance:

In Latin, in French and in many other languages, the present tense can be translated into English *either* by the *present indefinite* tense *or* by the *present continuous* tense. That is to say, the Latin *amo* and the French *j'aime* can be translated by "I love" or "I am loving." Indeed, they can also be translated by "I do love." Grammarians do not normally give a name to that last version of the English present tense, so for convenience I shall call it the *present emphatic* tense. It is of course almost always used in the negative, with "I do not like it" being much more common than "I like it not."

Similarly with the past tenses. In Latin, the *imperfect tense* describes actions or states not completed or going on over a period of time, or again and again; and it can be translated *either* as in (a) "I was loving grammar last year" *or* as in (b) "I loved grammar all last year." The *perfect tense* in Latin, describing actions which are completed or "perfected," can be translated as in *either* (a) "I have learnt all the grammar I need to know" *or* (b) "I learnt grammar when I was a child" *or* even (c) "I have been learning grammar all my life," the *perfect continuous tense.* And the *pluperfect tense* in Latin can be translated into English as in either "I had learnt" or "I had been learning." (The *pluperfect tense* represents something *doubly* in the past; that is to say, in the past before some other point in the past that is referred to.)

Similarly, too, with the *future* tenses. In Latin, the *fu-*

ture simple tense can be translated as in "I shall love" or "I shall be loving," *and* the *future perfect tense* can be translated as in either "I shall have loved" or "I shall have been loving." Note, by the way:

a. When making a *straightforward statement about the future*, the future simple tense in English is "I *shall* love," "you *will* love" and "thou *wilt* love" (in archaic English), "he/she/it *will* love," "we *shall* love," "you *will* love" (this time in the case of more than one person) and "they *will* love."

b. *Determination or emphasis* is indicated by the opposite to the above—"I *will* love," "you *will* love" and "thou *shalt* love" (in archaic English), "he/she/it *shall* love," "we *will* love," "you *shall* love" and "they *shall* love."

Thus:

a. The drowning man crying out "I shall drown, and no one will save me" is simply *foreseeing* what, to his regret, is going to happen.

b. The drowning man crying out "I will drown, and no one shall save me" is making it clear that he is *determined to* drown and not to be saved.

As will have been noticed above, many tenses, and also other parts of verbs, are formed by using auxiliary verbs—so called because they _help_ verbs to form some of their parts, as in "_am_ learning," "_do_ learn," "_have_ learnt." Some grammarians also include under this heading what are sometimes known as modal verbs. Modal verbs are for what are called _modal_ concepts, such as what is _possible_ (for instance, "can" and "could," "may" and "might"); what is _necessary_ ("must"); what is _allowed_ ("may" and "might" again); and what is _expected_ or _intended_ ("may" and "might" again and also "will" and "shall").

A substantial number of verbs, including many of those most commonly used, are irregular in the formation of their perfect tenses and also their past participles (see number 4.4 [b] [iii] below, on page 48). A list of these is given in Chapter 2 in Part III.

4.2. Voices. _Doing_ verbs are either in the active voice or in the passive voice. The _active voice_ of a _transitive verb_ is for when the subject of a sentence or clause is _doing_ whatever is being done, as in "I learn." (The transitive verb is defined and explained on page 69 and thereafter.) The _passive voice_ is for when the subject is not _doing_ the action but _experiencing_ it—that is, _having it done_ to him, her, it or them (as in "We are being taught").

4.3. Moods. Verbs are also either (a) in the indicative mood or (b) in the imperative mood or (c) in the subjunctive mood or (d) in the infinitive mood. The mood of a verb indicates its _function_—what it is being _used for_—in the sentence or clause in which it appears. That is to say, the mood of a verb reflects the speaker's *attitude* to what he or she is saying: for instance, whether he is taking it for a fact as to what either is happening or will happen or *has* happened; whether he is calling for it to happen; or whether he supposes that it might happen.

To be more technical, thorough and exact:

a. The *indicative mood* is usually for *making a statement* or *asking a question* (as in "I learn" and "Am I learning?"). Some grammarians would give a different mood for questions, the *interrogative mood*.

b. The *imperative mood* is (i) for *commands* (as in *"Stop!"*) and (ii) for when one *begs or entreats* (as in *"Help* me, please, if you can").

c. The *subjunctive mood,* sometimes in English and always in Latin and Greek and some other languages, is normally to be used when expressing *doubt, improbability, uncertainty,* an *order,* a *wish* or *recommendation,* a *condition* or a *purpose.*
   Examples:
   "If it *were* known that grammar was so important, more people *would* study it." In the indicative mood, that sentence would be "Since it *is* now known that grammar is so important, more people *are* studying it."
   "I *should do* it if I *were* you." Theoretically, the indicative version of that sentence would be "I

shall do it because I *am* you!"—but of course that means something different, since in that sentence I am mainly talking about *me* rather than about *you.*

"I have recommended to him that he *make* more effort."

"Resolved that the learning of grammar *be* everywhere promoted."

The idiomatic "If *need* be," "*Suffice* it to say" and "*Come* what may."

An important refinement of the principle governing the use of the subjunctive is (a) if what is being offered as a possibility is in fact not the case, the subjunctive should indeed be used; whereas (b) if it may or may not be true, the indicative must be used. Examples: (a) "If I *were* you, I should think carefully about this point of grammar"; (b) "If this book *turns out* to be useful to a reasonable number of people, I shall be glad that I wrote it."

d. The *infinitive mood* is used to express an action or state of being without giving any indication of a subject for the action or state (as in "to learn" and "to have been taught"). See also the next paragraph for a fuller explanation.

4.4. Non-finite parts of verbs. After tenses, voices and moods, there is one last group of verb parts that needs to be looked at: what are called the non-finite parts of verbs.

Non-finite parts are verb parts which, unlike all other verb parts, are not, and cannot be in any way, connected with a subject. There are three non-finite verb parts: the infinitive (as in "To teach"); the participle (as in "The *teaching* profession"); and the gerund (as in "*Teaching* is satisfying"). By contrast with the other verb parts, none of these can have a noun or personal pronoun placed in front of it as a subject. In more detail:

(a) The infinitive simply names the action or state without reference to who or what is either (i) *doing* the action or (ii) *being* whatever it is that he, she or it is being. Examples of infinitives are "to teach" (present indefinite active); "to be teaching" (present continuous active); "to be about to teach" and "to be about to be teaching" (future indicative active and future continuous active); "to have taught" and "to have been teaching" (perfect indicative and perfect continuous active); and "to be taught" and "to have been taught" (present indicative passive and perfect indicative passive—there is no continuous passive infinitive).

To split or not to split infinitives? Or perhaps: to freely split infinitives, to occasionally split them or to never split them? That last sentence shows what is meant by the split infinitive. The verb "to split" was split three times by interposing an adverb between "to" and "split" rather than putting the interposed adverb before or after "to split."

To use technical language, to split an infinitive is to put an adverb or adverb-phrase between the "to" and the verb, as in "to *ignorantly but, even so, outrageously* split an infinitive." It is increasingly being done and increasingly being defended, with "pedants" now often the category in which defenders of the traditional position are classified. Indeed, even most traditionalists accept that the split infinitive is now so widespread that in practice it has become an acceptable part of the English language.

The best arguments used by those who favour allowing the splitting go along the following lines. The objectors to splitting point out that much English grammar is based on Latin; the infinitive in Latin is a single word; and therefore in English the infinitive should be treated as effectively a single word. And that, the objectors continue, is simply not a good enough reason to avoid splitting when doing so would cause ambiguity or some other inconvenience.

The Latin-based reason, although indeed often used by supporters of no splitting, is however false and bordering on fatuous. Were that the reason not to split, we should be unable to split some of the English *tenses* either where Latin has one word and English has more—thus unable to do the following splitting: "I *am not splitting* infinitives now, and *have never split* infinitives in the past, and *am never going to split* infinitives in the future." The reality is that although Latin has of course influenced English greatly, English is at the root a Germanic language, and we have in fact inherited our "to" from the original equivalent of present-day German's *"zu";* and *"zu,"* although not as indispensable to the infinitive as our "to" is, often clings even more closely to its parent verb. Thus "in order to go out" in German is *"um auszugehen,"* equivalent to "in order out-to-go."

"Is it not sometimes necessary to split infinitives to avoid ambiguity or other awkwardness?" liberals may object. "For instance, in the sentence, 'Our aim is further to improve our grammar,' it is left uncertain whether an additional aim is intended or some additional improvement."

Certainly the problem of avoiding the split infinitive cannot always be solved by moving the word splitting the infinitive to a different place in the sentence or clause. It can, however, *always* be solved by a fairly minimal recasting of the sentence that makes no change to the meaning. "In nearly 30 years as a professional writer I have yet to find a context in which the splitting of an infinitive is necessary in order to avoid ambiguity or some other obstruction to proper sense," says Simon Heffer in his *Strictly English* (a book, published as recently as 2010, which carries my enthusiastic recommendation in "Further Reading"). Literary history confirms his judgement. Shakespeare never needed to split an infinitive,[*] and scarcely a single instance of a split infinitive is to be found in the classical authors of the last two centuries.

"Scarcely" rather than "never"?

---

[*] His "to pitied be" in "Thy pity may deserve to pitied be" in Sonnet 142, sometimes cited by splitting-infinitive promoters, is not a split infinitive, which, as noted above, involves the insertion of an adverb or adverb-phrase, but an inverted passive, a "switch around" for the sake of the metre and the rhyme. It is safe to say that the writer would not have done that in prose.

Yes, there is a significant exception among those most-read authors of the past. But it is a case of "The exception proves the rule," as the maxim tells us.

"But is the maxim right?" it may be objected. How can an exception prove a rule, rather than prove that it is not a rule after all?

Consulting any standard English dictionary will give the answer. According to my *Concise Oxford Dictionary,* the *primary* meaning of "prove" is not "demonstrate" but "put to the test." The word "prove" actually meant "test" in the days when that expression gained currency.

And the no-splitting-infinitives rule was indeed put to the test. A single well-known author, Fanny Burney of the late eighteenth and early nineteenth centuries, constantly split her infinitives. Her novels and diaries were widely read and enjoyed. They were praised by such eminent writers as Dr. Samuel Johnson and Edmund Burke. They were even an important influence on Jane Austen. Yet not a single writer of any significance imitated her in that respect. The rule was "proved"—was tested—as severely as could reasonably be thought necessary; and the unanimous judgement was, by implication, that it was a rule worth keeping.

My strong recommendation is that infinitive-spitting should never be done, other than, possibly, as an obviously intended "special effect," as in "I urge you to in absolutely no circumstances, whatever the provocation, split an infinitive." On the one hand, no one will object to the absence of split infinitives in your writing as long as you are careful to avoid awkwardness of any kind; and on the other hand, there will always be people who have read enough good literature of the past to find split infinitives inelegant, ugly or otherwise uncomfortable. There will therefore always be a possible cost without the prospect of any compensating gain.

(b) A participle is a part of a verb which does the job of an adjective as well as the job of a verb. It is called a participle because it *participates* in the natures of both verbs and adjectives. Other important facts about participles are:

    i. Sometimes a participle is simply a part of a tense, as in "I am *teaching*" (where "teaching" is the present participle) and "I have *taught*" (past participle).

    ii. There can be present or continuous participles that are *active* (as in "the *teaching* profession") and *passive* (as in "children are *being taught*").

    iii. There can be perfect participles that can be active and passive (as in "having taught" and "having been taught").

    iv. There is no actual future participle verb-form, but there are ways of expressing the equivalent of future participles. For instance:

        In "the world to come" or "the world that is going to come," the infinitive there is referring to some time in the future.

        In "I am about to master English grammar," the *near* future is indicated.

In "I am on the point of mastering grammar," the *immediate* future is indicated.

A participle can double up as both an adjective and a verb at the same time. In the sentence "*Having studied* his grammar hard, the boy passed the test," "Having studied" is an adjective participle referring to the boy, even though "the boy" is not in that clause, and "his grammar" is the object of the verb "Having studied." (See Chapter 7 for what a clause is.)

v. Any treatment of the participle should include an explanation of the frequent error in composition commonly known as the dangling participle. This has nothing to do with word forms, however, and belongs to the next chapter.

(c) The gerund, formed from the verb by adding "-ing," is a verbal noun; that is to say, the gerund is in one respect a verb and in another respect a noun.

i. When it is a noun: It can be the *subject* or *complement* in a clause (as in "*Seeing* is *believing*"); *and* it can be the *object* in a clause (as in "They like *learning*"); *and* it can be *governed by a preposition* (as in "You are good *at learning*").

ii. When it is a verb: It can be in the *present active* (as in "*Seeing* is *believing*") or in the *past active* (as in "*Having learnt* grammar is something to be proud of") or in the *present passive* or *past passive* (as in "*Being taught* grammar is not the same as *having been taught* it").

When the doing verb is *transitive,* the gerund normally needs an *object,* exactly as the many finite forms of the verb "do" (as in the last example in the last sentence). But note that it can be turned into a "pure" noun by using the preposition "of" to govern what would have been the object (as in "We relish the learning of grammar" instead of "We relish learning grammar").

One other piece of information about gerunds is worth noting, if only because it is the cause of so many people using incorrect grammar in relation to it. Because the gerund is a noun, it must be preceded by a *possessive adjective* ("my," "your," "his," etc.) rather than by a *personal pronoun* (such as "me," "you" and "him"). Thus, for instance, "Are you happy with the idea of *my* teaching you grammar?" is correct, and "Are you happy with the idea of *me* teaching you grammar?," which most people today would say and write, is incorrect.

Did you, dear reader, spot the error in that paragraph? I hope you did (though I *bet* you did not!), because I actually broke the rule that I was explaining *in the very paragraph in which I was explaining it.* The clause, "if only because it is the cause of so many people using incorrect grammar in relation to it," should of course read: "if only because it is the cause of so many people*'s* using incorrect grammar in relation to it."

Some grammarians, probably most today, would say that adding the correct grammar there would have the effect of making the sentence clumsy, making readers pause in order to try to work out what it is doing there and perhaps, with many readers, even to conclude that it is there by mistake, that there are times when grammar rules can be legitimately broken, and this is one of them. While granting the problem, I deny that solution, which, after all, is completely unnecessary. In my submission, the problem is better solved simply by rewording the rest of the clause, for instance, to "if only because it causes so many people to use" or "if only because it is the reason that so many people use."

(d) The gerundive, a verbal adjective, is a verb-form and usage which, to the best of my knowledge, has never appeared in any book of English grammar before—this despite its being used quite frequently in practice. It is a fairly important feature of Latin, with verbs in the gerundive carrying the meaning of "ought to be done," "fit to be done," and in old-fashioned English "meet to be done" (as in the schoolboy joke "lamb cutlets are meet to be eaten").

Without doubt, the gerundive is a useful concept, so much so that English speakers have long felt the need for it. But how could they set about introducing into our language a verb-form that does not exist and has no obviously practical way of being created?

Our resourceful ancestors found an admirable solution. They simply transported it straight from Latin without alteration, just as they imported "et cetera," "quid pro quo" and a multitude of other useful Latin expressions.

In Latin, verbs when in the gerundive end in *-andus* or *-endus* when they are describing single members of the male sex, in *-anda* or *-enda* when describing single members of the female sex, in *-andum* or *-endum* when describing single things that are neuter, and in *-anda* or *-enda* again when describing more than one thing that is neuter. In other words, the gerundive is declined like the adjective *bonus,* meaning "good."

Thus very much part of our everyday language are "memorandum," often shortened to "memo," meaning "what must be remembered," and the plural "memoranda" when there are several things to be remembered; "agenda," meaning "things that ought to be done"; the publishing terms "addendum" and "addenda" for one or more things that need to be added; and the political term "referendum," used for when decisions are referred to the electorate to be voted on directly rather than made by the government.

And I wonder how many ladies called Amanda and Miranda know that their names mean "worthy to be loved" and "worthy to be admired" respectively and were originally chosen for that reason.

4.5. Nouns derived from verbs. I do not intend here to give a complete treatment of the subject, but only to draw attention to a mistake that is constantly made in our day.

The endings "-er" and "-or" tacked on to the ends of

verbs are used to indicate that someone is *doing* the action in question. A "pay*er*" pays taxes, a "collect*or*" collects them, an "employ*er*" is someone who employs others and so on. Much less frequently, "-ee" is tacked on to the end of a verb when the action is *being done* to the person; it indicates what might be called a passive noun. A "pay*ee*" is someone who is or should be paid, an "employ*ee*" is someone employed and an "address*ee*" is addressed.

With crass illiteracy, the word "attendee" has come to be used to denote, not someone or something that *is attended,* but someone who *attends*—a conference or my grammar lessons or whatever. I have no hesitation in proscribing it ("proscribe" having the opposite meaning to "prescribe") as a usage to be fought. The word "attender" does not exist, though it would be legitimate to coin it, and "attendant" has different meanings from the one we need. "People attending" or ". . . who are attending, will attend or attended" some function is therefore the correct equivalent of the wrongly used passive noun.

4.6. Irregular verbs. Finally on the subject of verbs, there are the irregular verbs. Most verbs form both their past tense and their past participle by adding "-d" or "-ed" on the end of the base form. Thus "love," the base form of that verb, changes to "I love*d*" and "I have love*d,*" and the base form "wish" changes to "wish*ed*" in both cases. There are, however, more than two hundred verbs which do *not* simply add "-d" or "-ed" at the end, and they tend to be the more common verbs. We have already seen the remarkable example of what happens to the verb "to be." Other examples are "teach," "taught" and "taught"; "sing," "sang" and "sung"; "bet," "bet" and "bet"; and "go," "went" and "gone." A complete list of them is given in Chapter 2 in Part III.

5. Adverbs

An *adverb* is a word which modifies a verb, an adjective or another adverb. The word comes from the Latin *ad,* meaning "to," and *verbum* in its derived meaning of "verb." "Adverb" is therefore a sort of shorthand reflecting the fact that adverbs modify verbs much more often than they modify adjectives and adverbs. Adverbs are often the equivalent for verbs, adjectives and adverbs that adjectives are for nouns and pronouns.

The adverb should be placed as near to the word it modifies as possible. Compare "I hope you are *not only* finding learning grammar useful *but also* enjoying it" with "I hope you are finding learning grammar *not only* useful *but also* enjoyable." In the first sentence, "not only" and "but also" modify the verbs; in the second sentence, they modify the adjectives. There is of course no difference in overall meaning between the two sentences, but rather a slight difference of emphasis.

The main kinds of adverbs are adverbs of *time* (when,

as in "now" and "today"), adverbs of *place* (where, as in "here" and "there") and adverbs of *manner* (how, as in "quickly" and "slowly" and "easily" and "better"). There are also adverbs of number (as in "once" and "singly"), of degree ("very," "almost," "quite") and of reasoning ("therefore," "thus").

A few adverbs do not really fit into any category—examples are "however" (as in "*However* difficult grammar may seem at first"), "either" ("Don't you like learning grammar *either*?") and "just" (as in "Grammar is *just* so much fun"). In other words, "adverb" is another instance of where a *practically useful* definition is not technically an *adequate* definition.

Some adverbs are used to qualify whole clauses. In such cases, they either indicate that what the clause says is factual or otherwise (as do "probably," "presumably," "allegedly" and "actually") or indicate some sort of judgement on a fact (as do "surprisingly" and "admittedly").

Some adverbs, such as "carelessly" and "disgracefully," can play either role, and where they appear in the clause or sentence can determine their meaning. Thus "Disgracefully, he stopped working" means that it was disgraceful of him to stop, whereas "He stopped working disgracefully" means that his work started improving.

Any reference to the topic of adverbs which qualify whole clauses would be incomplete without some mention of two contentious points.

First, or—for the time being—firstly, is whether "first" or "firstly" is correct in lists continuing "secondly, . . . thirdly, . . ." and so on.

"The preference for *first* over *firstly* in formal enumerations," says H. W. Fowler in his, in general, justly revered classic, *A Dictionary of Modern English Usage,* first published in 1926,

> . . . is one of the harmless pedantries in which those who like oddities because they are odd are free to indulge, provided that they abstain from censuring those who do not share the liking. It is true that *firstly* is not in Johnson; it is true that De Quincey labels it "your ridiculous & most pedantic neologism of *firstly*"; the boot is on the other leg now; it is the pedant that begins his list with *first;* no-one does so by the light of nature; it is an artificialism. Idioms grow old like other things, & the idiom-book of a century hence will probably not even mention *first, secondly.*

Thus Fowler patronisingly and contemptuously dismisses two centuries of English literature, including two of the most erudite authors of the entire period, without producing a single comparable authority on his side and without showing the slightest interest in looking to any reasons that the traditional usage might have in its favour. It is surely not unfair to call the manner in which he treats the subject outrageous.

"One of the fetishes that used to affect a certain adverbial usage was that one wrote, in listing things, *first, secondly, thirdly,*" says, scarcely less scathingly, a book published within the last five years that, although by no means free from occasional errors, is for the most part so valuable that I feature it prominently in "Further Reading." "There was no logic to this," its author continues in the same authoritative tone.

"Either is OK, but be consistent in a list, so 'first, second and third'; or 'firstly, secondly and thirdly' (or even 'firstly, secondly and lastly'); but *not* 'first, secondly, third' (or 'firstly, second and last')," says a book, full of useful material, that was published just as I was on the point of sending this text to my publisher, going even further in proscribing the long-standing usage.

On the other hand, a book comparable to Fowler's *Modern English Usage* in its enduring influence and authority is Eric Partridge's *Usage and Abusage,* first published in 1942. And although Partridge must have been well acquainted with Fowler's book, that did not prevent him from laying down unequivocally: "Firstly is traditionally said to be inferior to first, even when secondly, thirdly . . . follow it."

Unsatisfactorily, Partridge's brief treatment gives no reasons to support his assertion: readers have to take it simply on his authority. I do not accept that a grammarian— or a writer in any other field—has the right to hold himself up as an authority on a disputed point.

For a satisfactory resolution, I bring forward my favourite of all of the dozens of books on grammar that I have consulted: Michael Dummett's *Grammar and Style: For Examination Candidates and Others,* published in 1993 and still in print, although remarkably little known.

> *First, secondly.* "First" can be either an adjective, as in "the first man on the moon," or an adverb, as in "He first filled the kettle and then put it on the stove." The form "firstly" is therefore as redundant as "fastly" would be, and should never be used. "Second," "third" and so on can only be adjectives. Hence an enumeration of points should proceed: "First, ... Secondly, ... Thirdly, ..."

Dummett's reasoning is clearly conclusive, on the basis of evidence that Fowler and his followers could have come up with simply by glancing through any of the standard English dictionaries of their day.

The second contentious point is the usage of "hopefully" that started creeping in about fifty years ago. Traditionally, its meaning was limited to "in a hopeful state of mind," as in "He set about his task hopefully," indicating that he was hopeful of success. Now it is widely used instead of "I hope" or "It is to be hoped," as in "Hopefully, you will benefit from reading this book."

Some modern books on grammar have wholeheartedly embraced it. "This book ... hopefully shows that good grammar, punctuation and spelling are more important than many people appear to think these days," say the joint authors of a well-publicised book on English grammar that was published in 2012. We know approximately what the authors mean, of course, because of the context, but the phrase leaves an impression of loose thinking. Do they hope that their book is convincing, or are they trying to be optimistic that their efforts to show that grammar is useful will bear fruit?

Happily—or rather, "I am happy to report that"!—this newish use of "hopefully" is not without opposition, even today. "Abandon 'hopefully,' all you who enter here," says the venerable *Times Literary Supplement* categorically in its instructions to its book reviewers, parodying the famous quotation from Dante's *Inferno*. Even more forceful is the experienced journalist Simon Heffer in his *Strictly English* (pages 84, 85): "This tiresome usage is now so ubiquitous that those who object to it are sometimes dismissed as pedants. It remains wrong, and only a barbarous writer with a low estimation of his readers would try to pass it off as respectable prose."

I hope, good readers, that you will join Dummett and me in the fight against "firstly" and Dummett, Heffer and me in the fight against "firstly" and "hopefully."

Moreover, while, same good readers, I am addressing you in this way, I may as well urge you to help stave off a corruption similar to "hopefully" that is taking hold: the failure to observe the distinction between "regretfully" and "regrettably." Only "regrettably" ("It is to be regretted that . . .") should be used to qualify a whole clause, but "regretfully" is increasingly being used as though it means "regrettably," reflecting the trend towards language becoming slipshod and therefore more indistinct in what it conveys.

Interestingly, in fact even remarkably—and those two are legitimate!—exactly the same wrong use of "thankfully" as that of "hopefully" has slipped into English language almost unnoticed and without protest.

Like adjectives, most adverbs can have comparatives and superlatives (as in "beautifully," "more beautifully," "most beautifully"). Adverbs are very often formed by adding "-ly" on to the end of adjectives (as in "quickly," but not as in "fast," "hard"* or "later," where the adverb has the same form as the adjective, nor in cases where the adjective already ends in "-ly," as do "friendly" and "lonely").

A special category of adverbs is used to form what are called compounded verbs. These verbs have words added after them to give them a specific meaning—for instance, "speak *up*," "put the candle *out*." The special meaning of such compounded verbs often seems arbitrary. Thus we "look *up*" words in a dictionary, we "look *out*" for gram-

---

* The adverb "hardly" does exist, of course, but only with the meaning "scarcely," which is not directly related to the adjective "hard."

matical mistakes, we "look *down*" on those who use bad grammar, we "look *after*" our copy of *Gwynne's Grammar* and we "look *for*" it if it is lost.

Great care is called for in this particular area of grammar, since some of the words added to compounded verbs are *adverbs* while others are *prepositions* (to be explained shortly), and it is not always easy to spot the difference since words such as "up," "in" and "on" can be either adverbs or prepositions according to context. To understand the difference, consider the following two sentences:

Amanda prudently looked *up* "gun-barrel" in the dictionary.
Amadeus imprudently looked *up* the gun-barrel.

Despite a superficial resemblance, the word "up" plays a quite different role in each sentence. In the first sentence, "up" is an adverb compounding with "look" to give it the special sense of consulting a reference book about something. In the second sentence, it is a preposition. You can easily tell the difference by trying out each expression in the imperative mood. The imperative will keep the preposition immediately before the object but can place the adverb elsewhere:

Don't look it *up,* Amanda! (*Adverb*)
Don't look *up* it, Amadeus! (*Preposition*)

6. Conjunctions

A *conjunction* is a word which joins together any two words of the same part of speech, or any two phrases, or clauses, or even sentences. It comes from the past participle *coniunctus* of the Latin *coniungo,* meaning "I join together."

I shall be saying more about conjunctions, in particular about what are known as co-ordinating conjunctions ("and," "both . . . and," "but," "or," "either . . . or") and subordinating conjunctions (all the rest of the conjunctions), in Chapter 8, "Punctuation," when we come to consider the rival uses of the comma and semicolon. In the sentence above defining "conjunction," incidentally, the first of the three "or" conjunctions joins together the noun-phrase "any two phrases" with the long noun-phrase "any two words of the same part of speech"; the second "or" conjunction joins the noun "clauses" to the long "any two words . . ." noun-phrase; and the third "or" conjunction joins the noun "sentences" to the same long noun-phrase. What this means will become clearer when we have learnt about phrases and clauses, including the distinction between main clauses and subsidiary clauses, during the course of Chapter 7.

Starting sentences with co-ordinating conjunctions is normally to be avoided, and in past times it was not uncommon for teachers to outlaw them completely. Although avoiding them is a good habit to form, exceptions to this particular rule can be legitimate when the writer knows what he is doing, and they serve a special purpose in an unusual situation. Whether or not *I* know what I am doing, you will find sentences starting with "And" here and there in this book, when it seems to be necessary.

7. Prepositions

A *preposition* is a word which governs a noun or a pronoun and connects it to anything else in the sentence or clause. For instance, "I teach grammar *from* my book *to* my pupils *in* my study *by* candlelight *with* pleasure." A preposition almost always stands *in front of* the noun or pronoun that it governs. This general rule can, however, be suspended if the result would be too clumsy, as in the famous example "This is something up with which I will not put," when "put up with" is obviously better.

Since prepositions can only do the job of governing nouns and pronouns, what are we to make of the sentence "*Until* recently you were not much good at grammar"?—or even "*Up until* recently you were not much good at grammar"?

The answer is that "recently" in that sentence has "magically" become a noun. There is confirmation of this in that the similar word "now" is listed in dictionaries as a noun as well as an adverb, and "now" clearly must be a noun in a sentence such as "Now is the time for every man to do his duty." Similarly, another word that is usually an adverb, "tomorrow," becomes a noun in "Tomorrow is another day," as dictionaries also recognise. And there is no difference between those "noun" uses of the words "now" and "today" and the use of the word "recently" in the sentence above. What is deceptive about "recently" is the "-ly" at the end.

A crass illiteracy on a par with "attendee," which we met above under the heading "Verbs," is "per capita," supposed to mean "per head." *Capita* is the plural—accusative plural in this case—of the Latin noun *caput,* meaning "head." When used in this sense, "per" is necessarily followed by a singular noun, whether the noun is an English one. "Per head," we say correctly, as also "per month" and "per year," which is *per annum*—singular—in Latin, not *per annos. Per caput,* insists the edition of the *Concise Oxford Dictionary* that was in force from 1964 to 1976, followed in brackets by "& erron. *per capita.*" Let us fight the erroneous alternative remorselessly.

Under the same heading, "data" is sometimes treated as a singular noun. It is the plural of the Latin noun *datum,* and any verb of which it is the subject should course recognise that.

The word "preposition" is derived from the Latin *prae,* meaning "before," and *positus,* the past participle of *pono,* meaning "I place"—hence "placed before."

8. Interjections

An *interjection*—the only part of speech of which animals are capable!—is an exclamation. A more analytical definition: an exclamation is a word or group of words which expresses some feeling of the speaker or writer, and either stands as a sentence on its own or is thrown into a sentence and yet forms no part of the construction of that sentence. It is often followed by an exclamation mark (see Chapter 8). Examples of interjections: "Phew!" "Oooooooh!" "How amazing!" "Oh gracious me!" "His grammar, *alas!* is deplorable, but at least it is, *thank goodness!* gradually improving."

"Interjection" comes from the Latin *inter,* meaning "between" or "among" or "in or into the middle of," and, as in the case of "adjective," the past participle of *iacio,* meaning "I throw." One can see how the word eventually included the concept of an expression being "thrown in" amongst a group of other words, or even between two sentences, abruptly and without strictly belonging to them in any syntactical way. ("Syntactical"? Please refer back to the discussion of syntax in Chapter 5.)

Throughout this book, stress is placed on the need to learn the most important definitions by heart. Here, to close this chapter, is a traditional piece of verse which children especially can usefully learn by heart and then enjoy reciting. The definitions in the verse are no substitute for those given in the previous pages—not only are most of them incomplete but the last and most difficult of them is simply shirked! Even so, the verse is useful both for reinforcing the most basic features of the parts of speech, including helping to make sure that they are clearly and completely understood, and for training the memory in general.

A noun names person, place or thing—
A man, a town, a thought, a swing.
An adjective describes a noun—
Small shoes, bright eyes, new gloves, green gown
(And pronouns too, the next one down).
Use pronouns such as we, me, they
Instead of using nouns all day.
A verb says what we are or do—
They dance, she is, he laughed, it flew.
An adverb tells how things are done.
We quietly talk, they quickly run,
An interjection shows surprise,
As: Oh! how pretty. Ah! how wise.
Conjunctions are for joining things
Like clauses, phrases
And prepositions? What are they?
Oh dear! That's difficult to say!

∞

The Most Important Syntax Basics

A *sentence* is most comprehensively defined as a word or group of words expressing a complete statement, wish, command or question, whether as a thought or in speech or in writing. The written sentence can be defined much more simply, and just as accurately, as a group of words ending in a full stop (or period), an exclamation mark or a question mark.

Examples illustrating the first definition:

Statement: "I *love* learning about grammar." *Wish:* "Long live the queen!" *Command:* "Do this homework for tomorrow." *Question:* "May I please have some more homework to do?"

A *clause* is a group of words with a verb in it. It is derived from the past participle *clausus* of the Latin *clau-*

dere, meaning "to shut." A clause is an *enclosed* group of words, complete with its own subject and predicate (both of which are defined almost immediately below).

While we are about it, a *phrase* is a group of words *without* a verb in it. Examples of phrases are "in this room," a group of three words which together can take the place of the adverb "here"; and "at this time," which can take the place of "now." As can be seen from the definitions of "clause" and "sentence" given above, a clause may also be a sentence, and a sentence may also be a clause. They need separate definitions, however, because (a) a clause can also be only *part* of a sentence and (b) a sentence can consist of several clauses.

More on clauses, and also on phrases, later in this chapter.

The *subject* of a sentence or clause is who or what the sentence or clause is all about. The word comes from the Latin *sub,* meaning "under," and the past participle of a word we have met before, *iacere,* meaning "to throw." The subject is "thrown under" the mind—as, perhaps, a book might be, not very politely, thrown under your nose for you to look at.

The predicate of a sentence or clause is the rest of the sentence, apart from the subject. That is to say, the *predicate* of a sentence or clause is whatever is said about the subject. The word comes from *praedicatus,* the past participle of *praedicare,* meaning "to proclaim"—the predicate is what is *proclaimed* about the subject.

Predicates normally include a verb, at least understood.

A *doing* verb is either a transitive verb or an intransitive verb.

A transitive verb is a doing verb that needs a direct object.

The direct object is perhaps the most difficult of all grammatical terms to define really clearly, so here are no fewer than *three* definitions of it! Choose which one you prefer to learn by heart. As can be seen from the examples given above,

   i. The direct object is that which undergoes what the subject of the sentence or the clause does.

  ii. The direct object is the person or thing to which an action or feeling is directed.

 iii. The direct object is the person or thing directly acted on by the subject of a sentence or clause.

The word "object" is derived from the Latin *ob,* meaning "in front of," and, once again, the past participle of *iacere.* An object is "thrown in front of" the mind.

An intransitive verb is a doing verb that does not take a direct object, as in the sentence "I come and I go," where neither verb can have a direct object. With intransitive verbs, the doer's action *stops with the doer,* and involves no one and nothing else.

Some verbs can be either transitive or intransitive. For instance:

We can *transitively* eat food and *intransitively* eat to live.

We can *grow* food and *grow* in height.

We can *open* the door and the door can *open*.

Although "fly" and "walk" are normally intransitive, we can *fly* an aeroplane or a kite and *walk* a dog.

Note that an intransitive verb can sometimes *look* as though it is followed by an object which, however, is *not* in fact an object. This is explained later under the heading of "Adverb-phrases" just before the end of this chapter (page 80).

The *objects* (or, more precisely, *direct objects*—see below, page 72) of transitive verbs are in what is usually called the objective case (which does the work of the *accusative* case in Latin and indeed, with the help of prepositions, serves for the *genitive, dative* and *ablative* cases too). Note also:

English nouns do not change their form whether they are used as subject or object of their verb, but pronouns sometimes do. Thus in "I see *him*" and "The man *whom* I see,"

a. "I" is in the nominative case, the case used for the *subject* or its *complement* (see below, under "*being word*," page 73) in a sentence or clause, and

b. "him" and "whom," which are the objects in their clauses, are in the objective case.

The objective case is also used after prepositions, as in "I am learning a lot of grammar *from* him *to* whom I am listening." That, incidentally, is why the nowadays all-too-common "between you and I" is incorrect and should be "between you and me." What causes people to fall into the trap is that the preposition "between" is separated by a couple of words from one of the pronouns that it is governing. Those who make this mistake would never say "Look at I" or "Come with I." Also some find, for no good reason, that "me" sounds less refined than "I."

The objective case is also commonly used (a) when the pronoun is the *complement,* as in "It's me," and (b) after the conjunction "than," as in "You are better at grammar than him," even though strictly speaking both are incorrect and should be "It is *I*" and "You are better at grammar than he," respectively.

In Latin and Greek, and also in German, knowledge of the accusative and dative cases is of great importance with nouns and adjectives as well as with pronouns. So, for that matter, is the genitive case, indicating possession, represented in English by

a. the preposition "of" before the noun or pronoun in question—for instance, "the competence or otherwise *of* your teacher"; or
b. the letter *s* at the end of the word, either preceded or followed by an apostrophe—for instance, "your

teacher's competence or otherwise" in the case of only one teacher, and "your *teachers'* competence or otherwise" in the case of more than one teacher.

Note, however, that "it's" is not genitive but the colloquial shortening of "it is." Thus, "*It's* time for this discussion to arrive at *its* conclusion."

Although *objects* following *doing verbs* are normally direct objects, some verbs (such as "give," "show" and "teach") can be followed by both a *direct* object and an *indirect* object. An *indirect object* is a noun or pronoun only *indirectly* affected by the verb it follows. That is to say, whereas a *direct* object is the person or thing that the action of the verb is *directed at* (as in "He teaches *grammar*"), the *indirect* object is the person or thing *to whom* or *for whom* the action is done (as in "He teaches grammar *to me*" and "He bought some grammar books *for me*").

In English (though not in Latin and many other languages), care can sometimes be needed to identify which object is which, direct or indirect. In cases of doubt, the indirect object can always be identified by rewording the sentence or clause. For instance, in the sentences "I buy him a book" and "I give him a lesson," it becomes clear which of the two objects is the direct object and which one is the indirect object if they are reworded as "I buy a book *for him*" and "I give a lesson *to him*." In other words, if in doubt when there are two objects, try inserting the preposition "to" or "for" before each object in turn, and see if and when the sentence still makes good sense.

After a *being word,* what follows is *not* an object in the objective case (called the accusative case in Latin) but a complement in the same case as the subject, which is called the nominative case in Latin. This is especially important in Latin—thus, "I *am* a girl, and I *love* Latin" translates into *"Puella sum et lingu*am *latin*am *amo."* It does occasionally apply in English as well, though. Thus it is grammatically correct to say "It is *I*" rather than the colloquial "It's *me.*"

To explain the *complement* further, and to contrast it more clearly with the *object:* a collection of words such as "Grammar is" is incomplete. The *complement* is the part of the sentence or clause that is added to the *being word* to complete the sense. Yet another way of looking at it is that, in the case of a *complement,* it and the subject refer to the *same* person or thing, whereas in the case of an *object,* it and the subject refer to *different* people or things. (This rule is subject to a single exception: when the object is expressed by a reflexive pronoun. In the sentence "The teacher teaches himself" or "He teaches himself," both the subject and the object are of course the same person.)

Many words can be several different parts of speech, according to how they are used in any particular sentence or clause. Examples are:

a. The word "near." "Near" is:

An *adjective* in the phrase "a *near* relation."

An *adverb* in the sentence "Please stay *near* at hand."

A *preposition* in the sentence "Please come and sit *near* me."

A *verb* meaning "draw near to" or "approach," as in the sentence "Soon we shall *near* the end of this lesson on 'near.'"

A *noun* in the sentence "'*Near*' is a word that can be an adjective, an adverb, a preposition, a verb or a noun." (But any word becomes a noun when we are talking *about* the word rather than *using* it.)

b. The word "before." "Before" is

An *adverb* in the sentence "Have you been here *before*?"

A *preposition* in the sentence "You go *before* me and I shall follow."

A *conjunction* in the sentence "Did you arrive *before* I did?"

A *noun* in the sentence "'*Before*' is a word that can be an adverb, a preposition, a conjunction or a noun."

Clauses (groups of words with verbs in them) and phrases (groups of words *without* verbs in them) need further examination.

There are two main kinds of clauses: main clauses, which are sometimes called *independent* clauses, and subsidiary clauses, which are sometimes called *dependent* clauses. *Subsidiary clauses* are introduced by conjunctions or relative pronouns, at least understood, though not always actually included. Examples: "He said [that] he didn't like learning about grammar," where "that" (understood) is a conjunction; and "Unfortunately, he couldn't know the important grammar [that] he should have been taught but never was," where "that" (understood) is a relative pronoun.

By contrast with *main* clauses, *subordinate* or *dependent* clauses cannot be sentences by themselves.

Some examples illustrating what has just been said about main and subsidiary clauses:

a. "You are learning English grammar, and English grammar really is important and useful" is a sentence consisting of two main clauses—each clause can make complete sense by itself.

b. In the sentence "You are learning English grammar because English grammar is important and useful," the second clause is a subsidiary clause, depending on the first clause to make sense.

c. In the sentence "You are learning English grammar because English grammar is important and useful, as everyone would agree if everyone were [subjunctive—see pages 42, 43] prepared to take the trouble to study the subject properly":

  i. The *third* clause ("as everyone would agree") is subsidiary to, and dependent upon, the subsidiary clause immediately in front of it ("because English grammar is important and useful").

  ii. The *fourth* clause ("if everyone were prepared to take the trouble to study the subject properly") is subsidiary to, and dependent upon, the third clause or second subsidiary clause ("as everyone would agree"). In other words, the fourth clause ("if everyone were prepared to take the trouble to study the subject properly") is a sub-sub-subsidiary clause!

Subsidiary clauses deserve special attention. This is because, as the student gets to the advanced stages of learning English and other languages, and all the more so as he or she gets to the more advanced stages of learning classical Latin and Greek, learning to handle correctly and effortlessly the various types of subsidiary clauses is the most demanding and time-consuming task of all.

Incidentally, in this context, surely one of the most brilliantly constructed sentences with multiple subsidiary clauses ever written, with its deceptive appearance of effortlessness and simplicity, is this one by the twentieth-century humorous writer P. G. Wodehouse, who was revered by such eminent fellow authors as Hilaire Belloc and Evelyn Waugh as the greatest prose-craftsman of their time:

> With the feeling, which was his constant companion nowadays, for the wedding was fixed for the fifth of July and it was already the tenth of June, that if anyone cared to describe him as some wild thing taken in a trap, which sees the trapper coming through the woods, it would be all right with him, he threw a moody banana skin at the loudest of the sparrows, and went back into the room. (*Money in the Bank*)

Clauses and *phrases* perform the function of three of the parts of speech that have been defined in Chapter 6: nouns, adjectives and adverbs. There can therefore be noun-clauses and noun-phrases, adjective-clauses and adjective-phrases, and adverb-clauses and adverb-phrases, which do the work of nouns, adjectives and adverbs, respectively. Examples:

a. The sentence "*Learning Latin and English grammar* makes me feel *under the weather*" starts with a noun-clause, which is the subject of that sentence, and ends with an adverb-phrase, which modifies the verb "feel."

b. The sentence "*The girl with the happy smile* is *over the moon* at the exciting thought *of reading a book which teaches English grammar*" has (i) a noun-phrase ("The girl with the happy smile"), (ii) an adjective-phrase ("with the happy smile," describing the noun "girl"), (iii) another adjective-phrase ("over the moon," describing the noun-phrase "The girl with the happy smile"), (iv) an adjective-clause ("which teaches English grammar" describing the noun "book"), (v) a noun-clause following the preposition "of" ("reading a book which teaches English grammar"), and (vi) an even longer noun-clause following the preposition "at."

Noun-clauses are straightforward. Apart from what has been said about them above, it only needs to be noted that they are often reported speech of one kind or another. Examples:

Reported *statements:* "He says *that he will greatly benefit from learning grammar*"—instead of the direct statements "He will benefit from learning grammar," "He will probably benefit from learning grammar," etc.

Reported *commands:* "She demanded *that I teach her grammar*"—instead of the direct "Teach me grammar."

Reported *questions:* "They asked *if they could learn grammar*"—instead of the direct "Can/may we learn grammar?"

Reported *exclamations:* "We all realise *how important learning grammar is*"—instead of the direct "How important grammar is!"

Adjective-clauses are also straightforward. They are usually called *relative clauses,* and they are introduced by the relative pronouns "who," "whom" (including "of whom," "by whom," "with whom," etc.), "whose," "which" and "that." In English the relative pronoun can often be "understood" and left out, as in the sentence "Grammar is the subject I am studying now" instead of the more exactly correct "Grammar is the subject *that* I am studying now." In Greek, Latin and most modern European languages, the relative pronoun can never be left out.

Adverb-clauses are more complicated. Although, as noted on pages 54 and 55, adverbs can be divided simply into adverbs of time, adverbs of place and adverbs of manner, *adverb-clauses* have several more divisions. These are especially important in classical Latin and Greek, and indeed mastering adverb-clauses is the main difficulty in reaching the final stages of becoming really competent in those two languages. The most important kinds of adverb-clauses are:

Adverb-clauses of time: "I went away *before he arrived*" and "*When she got there,* the lesson started."
Adverb-clauses of place: "I found my grammar notes *where I had left them.*"

Adverb-clauses of manner: "He recited the Latin verb *'amo' as he had been taught to.*"

Adverb-clauses of reason: "*Because you are doing your best,* you can expect to pass the test."

Adverb-clauses of purpose: "She worked hard *so that she would pass the test.*"

Adverb-clauses of result: "We all worked so hard *that we passed the test.*"

Adverb-clauses of condition: "*If they had worked harder,* they would have passed the test as well."

Adverb-clauses of concession: "*Although I did no work at all and did not deserve to pass the test,* I somehow scraped through it."

Adverb-clauses of comparison: "I found the test *easier than I had expected to find it.*"

Adverb-phrases. It is worth noting that *adverb-phrases* can be used in the same way as *adverb-clauses* can.

A few examples based on the examples of clauses given above:

Time: "I went away *before his arrival.*"

Reason: "*Because of your hard work,* you can expect to pass the test."

Manner: "I passed the test *quite easily.*"

One trap with adverb-phrases, and also with adverbs, has already been mentioned but not yet explained. Adverbs and adverb-phrases can sometimes *look* like nouns and noun-phrases and therefore superficially make intransitive verbs *look* like transitive verbs. To illustrate this, in the sentence "I arrived home after I had walked a long way":

a. The word "home" is *not* a noun (and therefore *not* the object of the verb "arrived," which therefore has *not* suddenly become a transitive verb). It is an *adverb* modifying the verb "arrived." This can be more easily recognised if the word "home" is expanded into "at my home," which of course means exactly the same, does the same job in the sentence and is clearly an adverb-phrase. It can perhaps be recognised even more clearly if "home" is exchanged for another word which means something slightly different but does the same job, such as "here" (in "I arrived *here*").

b. The phrase "a long way" is *not* a noun-phrase (and therefore *not* the object of the verb "walked," which has not stopped being an intransitive verb). It is an *adverb*-phrase modifying the verb "walked." This can be more easily recognised if the phrase "a long way" is lengthened into "*for* a long way," which of course means exactly the same, does the same job in the sentence, and is clearly an adverb-phrase.

That is all that needs to be said about *adverb-phrases.* By contrast with adverb-*clauses,* adverb-*phrases* and their construction involve few difficulties.

Sequence of tenses, which is important in English and even more so in Latin and Greek. What *sequence of tenses* means is that there must be a sort of *agreement* between the tense of the verb in the *main* clause and the tense of the verb in any *subsidiary* clause. Therefore, for instance:

a. "I *say* that I *am* not finding learning grammar desperately difficult" uses the *present* tense in both clauses.
b. If, however, the words "I say" in that sentence are put into the *past* tense, the words "I am" must *also* go into the past tense, and the sentence must become: "I *said* that I *was* not finding learning grammar desperately difficult."

A difficulty with this sequence-of-tenses principle is that the *past* tense in the subordinate clause often refers to the *present* time, as in "It is a pity that the new-fangled teachers *did not realise* that grammar *was* such an important subject." In reality, what "the new-fangled teachers" did not realise of course is that grammar *is* such an important subject. The word "was" in that sentence is used in order to make the tense of the verb in the subordinate clause agree with the tense of the verb in the main clause.

When, as here, the sequence of tenses rule has the result of making the meaning unclear, it is as well to reword the sentence, for instance in that case to "did not realise the great importance of grammar."

CHAPTER 8

Punctuation

Punctuation of course applies only to written work. Accurate knowledge of punctuation can, however, be essential to the understanding of written work, because different punctuation can completely change the meaning of a sentence, as we shall see shortly.

English punctuation consists of: full stop (in America, period); colon; semicolon; comma; question mark; exclamation mark; inverted commas (in America, quotation marks); apostrophe; brackets of two kinds—round brackets (in America, parentheses) and square brackets (in America, just brackets); hyphen; dash; ellipsis; what is sometimes called slash and sometimes oblique; and, not strictly a punctuation mark but we must learn about it somewhere, asterisk.

Briefly, and far from completely:

The full stop, from now on in this edition the period. The most important use of the period is to show the close of a sentence, as at the end of this sentence. It is also used to indicate abbreviations, and while this used to give rise to no difficulty because any kind of abbreviation always ended with a period, that is no longer so. From the 1950s onwards, it was being argued in England, though not in America, and largely unsuccessfully even in England, that it should be abolished in some circumstances. Now most writers in England omit it, but I am happy to say that most writers in America do not. Even in America it is commonly omitted when initials are used by themselves to represent, in effect, a full name, as do JFK and LBJ. Other instances where it is omitted in America are when abbreviations of names or titles are exclusively or all but exclusively capital letters, as with US, UK, NY, VP, CEO, MD, and even PhD. More on this below.

Because the omission of the period in every abbreviation is so widespread and seldom gives rise to ambiguity, I think it as well to be compromising for the second time in this book. What I shall do is give the relatively few rules for where the period should be kept by those who still keep it in some cases but not others, while making it clear that these rules are quite commonly broken in both directions—on the one hand, by people who never use the period at all for abbreviations, and on the other hand, by people such as me who keep to the practice which was still the most common one thirty or forty years ago and is probably still the most common one in America today, that of using the period for all abbreviations.

My authority for what follows is the 1964 to 1976 edition of the *Concise Oxford Dictionary,* the most popular of the smaller Oxford dictionaries. (In 1976, a massively revised edition was published, to be followed by no fewer than five further editions up to the present time.) This dictionary expressly states that, at the time that it was setting down these rules, in 1964, it was more usual for all abbreviations to have the period.

1. If after the first one, two, or more letters of a word, the word is then cut short, it is cut short with a period. Examples: "N." for "North," "pron." for "pronoun" and "abbrev." for "abbreviation." Included in England would be "Yorks." for "Yorkshire" and "Leics." for "Leicestershire," to show that the *s.* represents "shire." In America, one would have "Conn." for "Connecticut" and "Fla." for "Florida." The only exceptions to this rule are abbreviations in mathematics, such as "sin" for "sine," "cos" for "cosine" and "tan" for "tangent."

2. If some portion of the middle of the word is left out, with the first and last letters being kept, the period at the end can be left out. Examples: "hrs" for "hours" and of course "Mr" and "Mrs," common in Britain, although not used in America. To be fair to this usage, which, as I say, I have not adopted

myself, ambiguities caused by omissions are rare,
"caps" for "capitals" (capital letters) being the most
obvious one.

3. There is a mixed group: two or more words together
   in a phrase, most usually a Latin phrase. Examples
   are "e.g." (*exempli gratia* or "for example"), "a.m."
   (*ante meridiem*) and "p.m." (*post meridiem*), and
   "B.C." ("before Christ") and "A.D." ("anno Domini"
   or "in the year of Our Lord"), and of course
   "U.S.A.," this last one at least now sometimes
   written without the periods.

It is worth drawing attention to one remarkable effect
of rules (1) and (2) being used together, which the *Concise
Oxford Dictionary* expressly mentions. If those rules are
followed consistently, the abbreviations of American states
such as Massachusetts ("Mass.") and Oregon ("Oreg.")
must include the period, while the abbreviations of some
others, such as Virginia ("Va") and Kentucky ("Ky"), must
exclude it.[*] Consistency of applying the rule produces a
similar inconsistency with the measurements "inch" ("in.")
and "foot" ("ft"). It is easy enough to see why the mixed
use of the period for abbreviations was unlikely to last. For

[*] For organisational simplicity, the United States Postal Service
does in fact abbreviate the names of states down to two capital letters and without the period, as in MA for Massachusetts. Abbreviations for other purposes, however, commonly keep the period, as
on signposts giving "The Mass. Pike" to indicate the Massachusetts
Turnpike.

me, the same reason persuades me to stay with the system which caused no difficulty or inconvenience over a period of centuries.

The comma. At the opposite extreme from the period, the comma represents the shortest pause inside a sentence and is often used instead of conjunctions to divide (a) the same parts of speech when one occurs immediately after the other, (b) phrases and (c) clauses. Examples of some of these uses in a single sentence: "My pupils, whether they are young children, older children or adults, are expected to try to be painstaking, accurate and stylish at reading, writing and declaiming English, Latin and even, in some cases, Greek."

Other uses:

a. In place of "and" (as in "I am teaching, you are learning, and we are both hoping for the best").
b. Immediately after addressing someone (as in "Good reader, are you paying attention?").
c. After one or two introductory adverbs, sometimes almost used as conjunctions (as in "At length, however, . . ."—in that case, an adverb-phrase followed by an adverb).
d. In lists. Here in England, though most often not in the United States, the comma should normally be left out of the last item of a list if it is preceded by "and." Example: "The most frequently used

punctuation marks are the period, the comma, the colon, the semicolon, the question mark and the exclamation mark." Even in England, the comma should be included in the following cases:

i. If one of the items involved has an "and" in it. Example: "The most frequently used punctuation marks are the period, the comma, the colon, the semicolon, and the question and exclamation marks."

ii. If the list is made up of clauses that are so long that a comma will make it easier for the reader to see where one clause ends and the next one starts. Example: "I am trying to teach you English grammar, you are not trying hard enough to learn it, and we are both getting fed up."

   When a comma is included in such lists without the need provided by the additional "and," it is known as the Oxford comma (often—perhaps competitively!—called the Harvard comma in America). This would usually be considered bad English in British English but is the normal usage in American English.

e. Finally, we must look at commas used in pairs, sometimes called bracketing commas. And it is worth making the general point that of all punctuation the importance of the correct use of the comma is especially worth noting and studying, since using it or leaving it out can give *radically* different meanings to sentences which are in every other way identical. Examples:

1. My brother, who lives in London, is a teacher of grammar.
2. My brother who lives in London is a teacher of grammar.

   In the first sentence I have only one brother; in the second, more than one brother.

1. Politicians who tell lies are to be despised.
2. Politicians, who tell lies, are to be despised.

   In the first sentence only *some* politicians are to be despised; in the second sentence, all of them.

1. This morning he had a grammar lesson, which was very unusual.
2. This morning he had a grammar lesson which was very unusual.

   In the first sentence, it was very unusual for him to have a grammar lesson, or possibly very unusual for him to have a grammar lesson on this particular morning (the sentence is slightly ambiguous in this respect). In the second sentence, he had a very unusual kind of grammar lesson.

Note: In American usage it is standard
practice to introduce restrictive clauses with
"that" and non-restrictive clauses with "which."
This is only legitimate in the UK; not obligatory.
Therefore, in the second example above, in which
a restrictive clause is used, American writers
would normally substitute "that" for "which" so
the sentence would read: This morning he had
a grammar lesson that was very unusual. That
would be acceptable in the UK as well, but, as I
say, by no means necessary.

How do we decide when to use the commas and when
to leave them out? In technical language, the commas
must be (a) omitted when the relative clause in question is a restrictive relative clause and (b) put in when
it is a non-restrictive relative clause. Exactly what these
clauses are and do, and why the one is used without surrounding commas and why they are needed for the other,
is explained in different ways in various good books on
English, including Professor Strunk's little masterpiece reproduced in Part II. Let me see if I can come up with yet
another explanation: one that is so clear that none of my
readers can ever be in any doubt.

A restrictive clause—perhaps defining clause, used by
some grammarians, is a more clearly descriptive term—is
so closely bound up with the noun or noun-phrase it is describing that its use there *restricts* the meaning of—gives

a special meaning to—that noun or phrase, and it cannot be left out without an essential part of the meaning of the noun or noun-phrase that it is describing being lost. So much is this so that although one would not do so in practice, one could theoretically hyphenate together every single word from the beginning of the noun or noun-phrase to the end of the restrictive clause. Thus, "My-brother-who-lives-in-London is a teacher"—which of course leaves no room for a comma after "brother." Without the restrictive clause attached to its noun or noun-phrase, the sentence would make either no sense or a completely different sense from what the writer intended.

A non-restrictive clause—sometimes called more descriptively a commenting clause—is a clause which, in effect, makes a separate statement within the sentence about the noun or noun-phrase. It could be left out without the essential meaning of the sentence changing. Indeed, the commas surrounding it perform the same function as brackets would—hence the term "bracketing commas" that is sometimes used. Thus, in the sentence "My brother (who lives in London) is a teacher," commas or brackets are *necessary* for the correct sense of the sentence.

One last thing to remember about these two different kinds of clauses is that where there is a choice between "that" and "which" to introduce a clause, "that" should usually be used to indicate restrictive clauses and "which" to indicate non-restrictive clauses. Please note that I carefully said "should *usually* be used to indicate restrictive clauses" rather than "should *always* be used." Although "that" is strictly correct there, even good writers sometimes use "which"—as alert readers may have noticed that I myself did when defining the restrictive clause in the previous paragraph, and indeed in many of the definitions in this book.

The colon introduces (a) direct speech in quotation marks (see below, page 97), (b) a quotation, or (c) a list of examples or particulars (as in "I am learning the following: English, Latin and Greek"). The comma is now very often—perhaps more often than not—used in front of a quoted sentence in place of the colon. I am against this, as is the *Economist*'s best-selling manual, *Style Guide.*

The semicolon, indicating a longer pause than does the comma, is used

a. when two or more sentences are thrown into one, for reasons either of sound or of sense (as in "I think you are wrong; you may be right");

b. to separate rather lengthy main clauses (you will find many examples of this usage in this book);

c. to separate subsidiary clauses which, in succession, depend on the same main verb (as in the very sentence you are reading now, in which all the subsidiary verbs depend on the verb "is used," immediately before the (a), (b), (c) . . . lettering starts);

d. to divide clauses which are connected by a conjunction which either
   i. indicates an alternative (as in "Pay attention; *otherwise* you won't learn anything") or
   ii. indicates an inference (as in "I am hoping that you are paying attention; *for* this information about punctuation really is important").

Another use of the semicolon is when words, phrases or clauses would normally be separated by commas but there are other commas in the sentence doing a different job, as in "The pupil is learning English, of course; Latin, traditionally considered almost as important as English; and Greek."

Conjunctions again. Now that we know something about both commas and semicolons, we must turn back to the subject of conjunctions for a little more than could be suitably offered on this subject back in Chapter 6, page 62.

Conjunctions fall into two categories: co-ordinating conjunctions and subordinating conjunctions. Co-ordinating conjunctions are "and," "but," "or," "nor" and even sometimes—especially in American English—"yet." In the use of them that we are considering here, they connect to each other *clauses of the same rank,* whether *main clauses* or *subsidiary clauses.* By contrast, subordinating conjunctions *connect subsidiary clauses to main clauses and subsidiary clauses to higher-ranking subsidiary clauses* (that is, subsidiary clauses which they modify). Examples of these are "after," "before," "because," "as," "for" (when it means "because"), "since" (in both its meanings as a conjunction), "although," "in order that," "unless," "until," "while," "when," "whenever," "where," "wherever," "why" and the relative pronouns "who" and "which."

Rounding off our examination of commas and semicolons. Now, against that background, here are some important punctuation principles (principles that I have frequent struggles to get some of my pupils to remember!):

1. Unless they are part of a series of *more* than two main clauses, two main clauses may never be joined by a comma. Therefore,
   a. "I am trying to teach you English grammar, you are not trying hard enough to learn it" is not legitimate.
   b. "I am trying to teach you English grammar; you are not trying hard enough to learn it" is legitimate.
   c. Repeating exactly an example of a few pages back, "I am trying to teach you English grammar, you are not trying hard enough to learn it, and we are both getting fed up" is also legitimate.
2. As already mentioned, semicolons rather than commas between clauses in a series of equal-ranking clauses are at least desirable when some of the clauses *themselves* contain commas.

3. As already indicated a little earlier, a comma rather than a semicolon should almost always be used between clauses of unequal rank, when a main clause is followed by a subsidiary clause, or a subsidiary clause by a sub-subsidiary clause. Thus: "I have decided not to give up my struggle to learn English, although I am finding it dauntingly difficult, because there seems to be so much to learn." Some grammarians allow occasional exceptions before the conjunctions "since," in its causal sense, and "for"—as in "I was truly delighted to get your message; for it has been a long time since we were last in touch." The guide for this use of the semicolon is when the second clause indicates a striking contrast.

So much for commas and semicolons. As already indicated in an example given when the word "sentence" was defined at the beginning of Chapter 7, a question mark is used at the end of a sentence to show that the sentence is a question. It is also used inside a sentence when *part* of the sentence is a question (as in the sentence "'What is a question mark?' is now a question that you do not need to ask").

The exclamation mark is used both after words inside sentences and also at the end of sentences: (a) to show surprise or wonder (as in "Extraordinary! How astonishing!"); (b) to express emotion; (c) to show that the writer is intending to be funny or at least not as serious as the bare words would otherwise indicate; (d) to indicate sarcasm (as in "Oh, well done you!" when someone makes the same mistake for the third or fourth time). Care should be taken not to overdo the (c) use.

Inverted commas, or, almost always in the United States, quotation marks, indicate (a) the beginning and the ending of a quotation or of the actual words used by a speaker; (b) sometimes titles of books and articles; (c) sometimes slang; and (d) sometimes irony. Some writers, especially in the United States, ordinarily use double quotation marks; some single. Whichever is ordinarily used, the other should be used for a quotation or for anything else using quotation marks which occurs inside a quotation (as in "He sarcastically congratulated me on my 'hard work'").

The apostrophe is inserted:

a. To indicate the genitive, or possessive form, of a noun and of some pronouns. If it is placed *before* the genitive's *s,* it indicates that the noun is *singular,* as in "a girl's mother," as also in "one's," "anyone's" and "no one's." If it is placed *after* the genitive's *s,* it indicates that the noun is *plural,* as in "the girls' mothers." When the noun's ordinary plural does not have an *s,* the apostrophe goes in front of the genitive's *s* (as in "the children's parents").

b. To show that one or more letters have been left out of a word (as in "haven't," "won't" and both "it's" and " 'tis" for "it is").

   c. To denote the plurals of words that do not usually
      have plurals (as in "if's" and "but's," though "ifs"
      and "buts" is also completely acceptable);

   d. To denote the plurals of single lower-case letters
      ("Mind your p's and q's").

   e. Sometimes, though not usually in the United States,
      to denote the plurals of numerals ("What are two
      2's?"); and to denote the plurals of dates when
      the dates are written with numerals (as in "the
      1950's," though "1950s" is also acceptable). A classic
      illustration of the importance of the apostrophe is
      "Those smelly objects are my brothers/brother's/
      brothers'."

Round brackets, or parentheses, are usually for inserting something into a sentence that (although worth inserting, as in this case!) does not grammatically belong there.

Square brackets, or brackets, are mainly used for ex-
planatory or missing material added to a piece of quoted
text by someone other than the original author (as in "I
find it [this grammar-book] valuable").

The hyphen is used (a) to join two or more words
together when they become a single idea (as in "Hard-
to-tolerate early-morning noise-levels in almost-full classrooms normally used only by ten- to twelve-year-olds");
(b) for compound numbers from twenty-one to ninety-
nine; and (c) of course at the end of a line to show the break

between two parts of a word which is divided where one line ends and the next line starts.

The dash can be used:

a. To introduce an elaboration or explanation of what has just been said in the sentence (as in "I am beginning to understand dashes—I am really beginning to understand dashes").

b. In the same way as brackets are used, in which case two dashes are of course needed, one at the beginning of the insertion and one after it.

c. For what might be called special effects (as in "I—er—don't think I can be bothered to study grammar—and that is all that I am prepared to say on the subject").

d. To indicate an interruption, as in this illuminating snatch of dialogue:

"To be or not to be—"

"For goodness' sake, *stop* regurgitating that rubbish!"

"—that is—"

"I said, stop regurg—"

"—the question."

The dash differs from the hyphen in appearance: the dash is longer. The "en dash" is as wide as the letter *n,* and the "em dash" is as wide as the letter *m.* Thus, you have

"-," "–" and "—," respectively. There is no space before or after either an en dash or an em dash. When typing with a computer or other machine that has no line long enough for a dash, but only a hyphen-length line, the effect of a dash can be produced conventionally with two hyphens in succession, again with no space before the two hyphens or after them.

The asterisk refers the reader to a footnote. A series of asterisks used to indicate that some words or clauses were left out. This is now more usually done by a series of dots.

The uses of slash/oblique include the indication of (a) alternatives, as in the fourth and fifth words of this sentence, as in "he/she should mind his/her own business" and as in "and/or"; and (b) occasional abbreviations such as "c/o" for "care of" on envelopes and "n/a" for "not applicable."

Three dots in succession indicate an ellipsis—that is, the omission of a few words in a sentence being quoted—to save space, as in "To be or . . . : that is the question." Or the three dots simply indicate a tailing off . . .

Incidentally, plenty of examples of all punctuation marks being put to practical use will be found in the pages of this book.

CHAPTER 9

Putting What Is Being Learnt into Practice

Many books on grammar, and most of them today, have exercises at the end of each chapter or section of a chapter, to give the pupil practice at what has just been learnt. None are included in this book, and the reason is of some interest. Experience shows that, although practice-exercises in a grammar textbook are useful up to a point, they are useful *only* up to a point—so much so that it can by no means be certain that they are worth the space that they would take up.

By that I mean that it is an interesting facet of psychology that students, probably especially—though not only—young ones, are only too capable of learning a new grammar rule, doing exercises on it without making any mistakes and then, in their ordinary writing, *continuing to break the rule as consistently as they had been breaking it before.*

Does this seem improbable? Here is a very experienced schoolmaster of the past, Lancelot Oliphant, in the first chapter of his *A Matriculation English Course,* confirming what I have found repeatedly in my teaching:

> Young people . . . may, for example, be able to punctuate with meticulous accuracy a piece of prose given them as a punctuation test, but fail to make adequate use of their knowledge of punctuation in their ordinary written work. They may be able to detect the most subtle grammatical errors in "sentences for correction," and yet unwittingly introduce those identical errors into the very next essay they write. Such undigested knowledge is of little use. You must not only possess the knowledge, but know when and how to apply it.

How is it that children can know what to do and yet not do it in practice?

In fact, this applies even more to adults than to children. The reason is summed up in the word "habit." As we all know from experience, any habit we form dominates us even when we recognise that what that habit "makes" us do is wrong. All bad habits, and, all the more so, mental bad habits, dominate our conduct until replaced by new habits. Indeed, traditional wisdom has it that it takes fourteen times longer to learn something correctly after having first learnt it incorrectly than to learn it correctly the first time. From this psychological insight, completely neglected in modern education-theory, two things follow: first, the importance of correct teaching from the start, for the sake of efficiency and saving of time; secondly, the evident fact that undoing what has been taught incorrectly, and substituting what is correct, will always need much effort. It can indeed be credibly argued that nothing in this entire book is more important than what is in this paragraph.

Against that background, we can now turn to being constructive. We can look at the question: if *how to use* the knowledge acquired must be learnt, as well as *acquiring* that knowledge, how is this to be done?

The answer, clearly, is that the student must embark on the *struggle* of thinking. For instance, rather than do exercises out of a book, the student should be asked (a) himself—or herself!—to do the thinking-up of examples of what has just been learnt, and (b) to make a point of including examples when he next produces an essay or other piece of written work.

In other words, rather than do an exercise in much the same frame of mind as when doing a crossword puzzle, the student must *engage* with the problem, aiming at making the new rule, in a sense, a *part* of him.

I exhort you, therefore . . .

Teachers: Get your pupils writing regularly, under
    your supervision. There is no substitute for at least

some daily writing, which includes conscientiously finding ways of using what has just been learnt, and continuing to do so under your supervision until what is at first a struggle becomes habitual and effortless.

Adult learners: Again, there is no substitute for daily writing in the way just described. Try to find someone to whom you can submit your writing so that it can be checked with an objective eye. Indeed, do feel free to ask me to help you to find someone, if you have difficulty locating someone exactly suitable.

All learners adult and young: Supplement your daily writing with careful reading of the best writers of English, not primarily for the purpose of enjoying what you are reading, but, in this instance, for the purpose of studying and absorbing *how* they do what they do, so that you can at once start putting it into practice.

Suggested authors for this purpose are: Rudyard Kipling, Hilaire Belloc, John Buchan, George Orwell and Evelyn Waugh, who can safely be considered to be leading prose stylists of the twentieth century. Regarded by some of the best authors of the last century as the champion of them all was P. G. Wodehouse, a sentence by whom I quoted admiringly in Chapter 7, page 77. He too can be usefully studied, but *only* for examining how he achieves his effects. To such an extent does he stand alone that any attempt to imitate his technique can only be expected to fail embarrassingly.

Incidentally, all those authors were competent Latinists and could never have reached their standards of craftsmanship if they had not been.

Once again, what are needed are regular, painstaking, systematic, properly directed efforts. They are needed for *any* worthwhile skill, including those learnt purely to give enjoyment, such as table tennis and chess. And to make this point for one last time, learning to think and communicate in speech and in writing is the most worthwhile skill of all.

CHAPTER 10

The Grammar of Verse-Writing*

Time was when even the most ordinary education included training in competence at writing verse. And a very long time it was, covering the entire history of secular literature from three thousand years and more ago right up to well into the twentieth century.

Our ancestors had compelling reasons for insisting that this was an important feature of education. "It is important for us to become acquainted with the laws of writing verse," says Professor Meiklejohn in his introduction to his treatment of the subject in his valuable book, *The English Language: Its Grammar, History, and Literature,* published

---

* In Chapter 5, I said that grammar has two main divisions: morphology and syntax. Also included under the heading of grammar are such elements of language as pronunciation and the history of whatever language is being examined.

towards the end of the nineteenth century. "First, because it enables us to enjoy poetry more. Secondly, it enables us to read poetry better. Thirdly, it shows us how to write verse; and the writing of verse is very good practice in composition—as it compels us to choose the right phrase, and makes us draw on our store of words to substitute and to improve here and there."

It was even held to be socially useful—for instance, simple messages of thanks can be made more memorable and attractive by putting them into verse, which has the added advantage of showing that trouble has been taken.

It is important to realise that to write verse in the tradi- *verse* tional way is within the capacity of everyone who can write at all. What it amounts to is expressing what one wishes to say in lines of a rhythm that is *regular.* This is done by repeating pauses and emphasised syllables in different lines. The mechanism for this—the mechanical arrangement of the pauses and stressed syllables, syllables being the units of verse—is called *metre.* Often *rhymes* are used, rhymes being the same sound repeated at suitable intervals ruled by the metre. Most often the rhymes come at the end of the lines, but they can come inside them, as in Noël Coward's "In tropical climes there are certain times of day," and often with rhymes at the end of some or all of the lines. Verse written in metre but without any rhyming is called *blank verse.*

Poetry is not quite the same thing as *verse,* and although everyone capable of writing anything can write verse, by no means everyone can write poetry. Poetry is verse with

Poetry

an elevation and depth of message and a musicality of language which some people are capable of producing and some people are not. Composition that is neither poetry nor verse is called *prose*.

To such an extent was verse-writing considered to be an indispensable part of any proper education that virtually all of the books on grammar of the past which aimed at any sort of comprehensiveness included a treatment of the subject. I open at random a selection of such books in my shelves: the one by Professor Meiklejohn already mentioned; F. J. Rahtz's *Higher English* (1907); J. C. Nesfield's *Manual of English Grammar and Composition* (1898; revised by F. T. Wood in 1964); Lancelot Oliphant's *A Matriculation English Course* (1928, revised in 1948). All of them have substantial sections on "prosody," the technical name for the writing of verse.

Let it be emphasised: lines in accordance with regular, pre-determined rhythms, sometimes with rhymes at the end of them, *were the indispensable basis of all poetry*. Without regular metre, anything written or spoken simply was not poetry. "Rhythm is not *confined* entirely to poetry," says Rahtz in *Higher English*. "In poetry, however, the rhythm must be regular." Even standard dictionary definitions excluded what is called "free verse" from falling into the category of poetry. "Elevated thought or feeling *in metrical form*" (my emphasis) is how the *Concise Oxford Dictionary* defined poetry until 1976.

Then, after thousands of years of universal agreement as

to what poetry was, new light at last broke through, we are led to believe. Suddenly everything changed. Led mainly by Ezra Pound in the United States, and quickly followed by T. S. Eliot in England with *The Waste Land,* both metre and rhyming were abandoned, first by very few and then by more and more until where we are today, when they are scarcely to be seen today in published poetry. Indeed, the last prominent exponent of traditional verse was John Betjeman, Poet Laureate from 1972 until his death in 1984.

Because what I am going to say from this point on is inevitably controversial in today's world, it is important that I stress, as I have so often thought it necessary to do in these pages, that I am not putting forward personal subjective views of my own. Once again, I am not an innovator. On the contrary, my position throughout this book is that of defender and promoter of what has been shown to work over long periods of time and what is real. Furthermore, I am by no means the only person to have thought this position an important one to defend and promote. In the supposition that doing so will make my efforts to convey the message all the more convincing, I shall at this point let three eminent authorities on literature and one amateur who certainly knew what he was talking about speak for me.

Bevis Hillier, distinguished scholar, author and journalist, as recently as in *The Spectator* of 24 November 2012, in a passage especially valuable in that it includes eminent authors who speak with him:

> For me, Joyce and T. S. Eliot (and Ezra Pound, the evil genius of both) were the men who ruined literature . . . Eliot was a formidably good critic but mistook his vocation as a poet and pointed the way for all the drivelling, formless verse by others that the talented poet Peter Henham has called "a kind of messed-up prose."

"Messed-up" is actually a more seemly term than the one that Henham in fact used.

> Of Eliot's verse, G. M. Young wrote that it was "a gash at the root of our poetry." G. K. Chesterton wrote of free verse: "You might as well call living in a ditch 'free architecture.'" And W. B. Yeats, a poet far above Eliot, said that "poetry should be a dance in chains"— meaning that some rules and conventions should be adhered to.

That could hardly be more strongly worded. For a rather gentler look at the subject, I turn to an authority that Hillier has just quoted: G. K. Chesterton, one of the most popular authors of the twentieth century, on religion, politics, criticism of art and literature, even a writer of best-selling fiction (for instance, the Father Brown detective stories), and a poet in his own right. From an article by him called "The Problem of Free Verse," written in 1933, in which he examines a piece of free verse by D. H. Lawrence called "The Argonauts":

The first impression I have is that, while this mode of utterance has become free verse, it has not become free poetry. I mean that it has not produced any purely poetical effect that is freer or wilder or more elemental, magical, or hitherto uncaptured . . . It seems to me, I confess, that the actual effect of the feeling of liberty is even a certain limpness . . . [T]he practical problem of free verse [is that] of whether the freedom really does tend to liberty or only to laxity.

My third offering is by someone who, although he was one of the best-known entertainers in the world of his day, is, for our purposes, more of a man-in-the-street than the other three authorities that I am putting forward.

Richard Burton, notoriously one of Elizabeth Taylor's many husbands (twice over in his case) was intellectually much more than merely a film star. Early in his adult life, he had been accepted on a short-course programme at Oxford, and, as he later recorded in his diary, published only recently, he was always haunted by a sense of what he had missed because he took his academic education no further. Those six months at Oxford gave him a glimpse of academic seclusion for which he would hanker all his life, and he remained an addicted reader. Even when blessed by fame and fortune, he turned to books for solace, and what he wrote in his diary in May 1969 is as much worthy of being taken seriously as the observations of the others that I am quoting here:

I've decided that I don't know what poetry is. Last night, in a glut of gloom, I ploughed through the "collected" poetry, "all he wishes to preserve," of W. H. Auden. In ten thousand there is hardly one memorable line. Most of it is type-writing . . . Much of it is indifferent prose cut up . . . [And] listen to Yeats or T. S. Eliot . . . I think that once the mould of form was smashed by a master or series of masters, Pound and Eliot perhaps in poetry and the Impressionists even more perhaps (I know little about painting) in art, anybody can fool you. And will. And we will never know if they're mucking us about.

There Burton has got right to the point. By contrast with the traditional forms of poetry-writing, there is simply no possible way of distinguishing between modern free verse that is sincere and competently done and modern free verse that is either incompetent or foisted on a gullible public by someone laughing up his sleeve.

My final offering is from C. S. Lewis, who, remarkably, was a don at both Oxford and Cambridge and an author whose books sold widely whether he was writing literary criticism, novels, poetry, children's fiction (such as *The Chronicles of Narnia*) or Christian apologetics (most notably *The Screwtape Letters*). What he has to tell us on our subject is genuinely breath-taking. From his chapter "Donne and Love Poetry in the Seventeenth Century" in his book *Selected Literary Essays,* published by Cambridge University Press in 1969:

In discussing Donne's present popularity, the question of metre forces me to a statement which . . . will hardly be believed among scholars and hardly listened to by anyone else.

It is simply this—that the opinions of the modern world on the metre of any poet are, in general, of no value at all, because most modern readers of poetry do not know how to scan. My evidence for this amazing charge is twofold.

In the first place I find that very many of my own pupils—some of them from excellent schools, most of them great readers of poetry, not a few of them talented and (for their years) well-informed persons—are quite unable, when they first come to me, to find out from the verse how Marlowe pronounced Barabas or Mahomet . . . It is easy to find out that they have not got beyond the traditional legal fiction of longs and shorts and have never even got so far: they are in virgin ignorance. And my experience as an examiner shows me that this is not peculiar to my own pupils.

My second piece of evidence is more remarkable. I have heard a celebrated belle-lettrist—a printed critic and poet—repeatedly, in the same lecture, so mispronounce the name of a familiar English poem as to show that he did not know a decasyllabic line when he met it. The conclusion is unavoidable. Donne may be metrically good or bad; but it is obvious that he might be bad to any degree without offending the great body of his modern admirers. On that side, his present vogue is worth precisely nothing.

In other words, even among people reaching the highest level of education today, and all the more so today than back in the 1960s when Lewis was writing that, the introduction of free verse and the abandonment of traditional verse have all but universally eliminated people's ability to follow the rhythm of traditional poetry and to appreciate it. Yet this was an ability which any child used to have from his earliest years, as a result of reciting, or having recited to him, even such elementary trivia as the nonsense verses of Hilaire Belloc—such as "When George's Grandmamma was told / That George had been as good as Gold, / She Promised in the Afternoon / To buy him an *Immense* BALLOON"—and the even more nonsensical verses of A. A. Milne: "3 Cheers for Pooh! / (For Who?) / For Pooh / (Why what did he do?) / I thought you knew."

No one was better placed to know what he was talking about on that subject than Lewis, and what he said there fits in completely with what I have found in my own teaching and other experience. Under a certain age and, indeed, at a fairly advanced age, the average person today has not the faintest understanding of how traditional poetry works, let alone any understanding of how to compose it.

It is no exaggeration to say that this is a cultural disaster of gigantic proportions. What has happened is that one of the three great bodies of poetic literature of all time—I refer to the literatures of classical Greece and Rome and of the English-speaking world—has effectively been *completely cut off* from those who have inherited it, possibly forever.

If we need evidence that free verse leaves an unhappy gap in the inmost desires of human beings, and that metrical verse "speaks" to the most deep-seated impulses of all of us, it is to be found in the arena of song-writing by people who wish to be well rewarded in financial terms. While the "moderns" in poetry were triumphing everywhere during the last century, the popular song-writers were *not* following their lead. Whether we look at the lyrics written by Irving Berlin, Cole Porter, Johnny Mercer, Noël Coward, Lorenz Hart of the Rodgers and Hart team, Oscar Hammerstein of Rodgers and Hammerstein, Alan Jay Lerner of Lerner and Loewe, Lionel Bart, Timothy Rice of Rice and Lloyd Webber, the Beatles, the Rolling Stones or any other of the most successful lyricists of the last sixty or seventy years, *everywhere* we find the use of rhythm and rhyme. Rhythm and rhyme *sell.* They are what ordinary people *want.* They speak to our hearts.

Make no mistake: the authors just mentioned, who have made themselves fortunes by writing verse, have known *very* well where the money is, indeed on what their very livelihoods have depended. They have known as well as anyone that perfectly scanned and rhymed verse "speaks" to the mind and to the heart as formless verse, if verse it can be called, cannot begin to. They have known, too, that whatever time and effort were needed to achieve this perfection were well spent, since even small compromises momentarily distract attention and weaken the effect.

As so often, the occasional exception and apparent-exception serve to "prove the rule" in this instance, as a couple of examples will show.

Frederick Loewe of the Lerner and Loewe song-writing partnership, responsible, in their (and Bernard Shaw's) *My Fair Lady,* for one of the greatest musical-theatre successes of all time, in the song "On the Street Where You Live":

People stop and stare; they don't bother me;
For there's nowhere else on earth that I would
*   rather be.*

Notwithstanding the well-earned renown of Lerner and Loewe as songwriters, it is nevertheless true to say the slightly false rhyming of "bother" with "rather" would certainly interfere with the song's effectiveness for some listeners and that most of the other leading lyricists, of their contemporaries at least, would not have thought the use legitimate.

Lionel Bart in the song "Living Doll":

Got to do my best to please 'er, jest 'cause she's a—
*   living doll.*

That, by contrast, is completely legitimate, because the poem is in colloquial language throughout, and "jest" is an authentic substitute for "just" in the vernacular.

Similarly legitimate is this, in Noël Coward's "Mad Dogs and Englishmen":

because the sun is far too sultry,
and one must avoid its ultry-
violet ray.

Because Coward would not have considered it legitimate to try to get away with rhyming the "ultra" of "ultraviolet" with "sultry" (as some might well have done), he made a deliberate joke of falsifying the word itself for the purpose, with complete success.

I have now done my best to persuade my readers of the importance of this subject. It remains to make a small start in filling in yet another gap in today's education and culture. I shall give just a few of the most basic rules applying to English verse (not to the verse that was written in classical Greek and Latin, when rhyming had not yet been invented and rhythms were created in a different way) and leave the reader to pursue the subject with the help of one or more of the books listed in "Further Reading" or some other convenient source.

What follows includes a few technical terms to be added

to those that I have already given. There is no reason to be daunted by them. Although it is of course more important to *understand* what each one represents than to remember its name, nevertheless, as with any science—how to use computers is perhaps the most obvious present-day example—it is as well to learn the names of what we are talking about, if only for convenience.

These are the bare elements of English verse:

1. Verse is made up of *lines*. Each line has a fixed number of *accents* or *stresses* (for instance, the accent is on the first syllable of the words "accents" and "stresses"). Each accent has a fixed number of unstressed syllables attached to it, either immediately before it or immediately after it.

2. Each line is divided up into *feet*. Each foot consists of one accented syllable and either *one* unaccented syllable or *two* unaccented syllables.

3. The names of the different kinds of feet are as follows:

   a. An accented syllable with a single unaccented syllable in front of it is called an *iambus*. Examples are "perhaps," "inform" and "to be."

   b. An accented syllable followed by a single unaccented syllable is called a *trochee*. Examples are "teacher," "pupil," "lesson" and "Stop it!"

c. An accented syllable with two unaccented syllables in front of it is called an _anapaest_. Examples are "understand" and "get it right."

d. An accented syllable followed by two unaccented syllables is called a _dactyl_. Examples are "difficult" and "easily."

e. An accented syllable with one unaccented syllable on either side of it is called an _amphibrach_. Examples are "tremendous," "instruction," "I want it" and "I'm trying."

f. The _spondee_ consists of two accented syllables in succession. Although they occur often in some other languages, they seldom do in English, the only obvious instances being "maintains," "amen" and "farewell." They can easily be made up of two single-syllable words used together, though. Examples are "Good night," "Keep left," "Why not?"

4. Generally speaking, one can combine the anapaests with the iambuses and dactyls with trochees, and each of them with themselves alone, but not use any other combinations.

5. The most usual kind of verse in English is _iambic verse_. There are two kinds of iambic verse:

a. The _iambic tetrameter_, consisting of four feet. For example, "I wish to get this point across. / Ignoring metre causes loss."

b. The *iambic pentameter*, consisting of five feet. For example, "I've nearly finished setting out these rules," with the stress on the second syllable in every case. Much the greater part of English poetry was written in this metre, including all the blank verse in Shakespeare's plays and every line of his one hundred and fifty-four sonnets.

6. There are many other kinds of metre, as a glance through any compilation of traditional poetry will show. My purpose here, however, is merely to get the reader going in the right direction, rather than to come close to being exhaustive.

7. An important element of rhythm is what is called the *caesura* (which means "cut"), sometimes written as two vertical lines next to each other: ‖. The caesura is a break, or rest, in any line and is used at least in every line of four feet or more. Thus, in the first half of the first verse of Lord Tennyson's "Lady of Shalott": "On either side ‖ the river lie / Long fields of barley ‖ and of rye, / That clothe the wold ‖ and meet the sky; / And through the field ‖ the road runs by."

8. When lines of verse have regular rhythms, they are said to *scan*. When *we* are *scanning*, we are examining the number of syllables and feet of a piece of verse and identifying where the stresses are. (Our ordinary use of that word when we look

intently at someone's face or the horizon is a corruption of the original use in relation to verse.)

9. As already mentioned, much English verse includes *rhyming*—already defined above—as well as metre. Note there the inclusion of the word "sound": "rhymes being the same *sound*." What follows from that is that, much more than with prose, it is necessary to "read" poetry with one's ear, so to speak, even when doing so silently.

10. To be satisfactory, rhymes need to meet four conditions:

   a. The rhyming syllable must be accented. "Ring" can rhyme with "sing" but not with "teaching."

   b. The sound of the vowel must be the same, producing exactly the same effect on the ear, but not necessarily the spelling. Thus "lose" and "close" are hopeless rhymes, whereas "so" and "though" are completely satisfactory, and also "higher" and "fire."

   c. The final consonant must sound the same, though again it need not be spelt the same. Thus "mix" and "tricks" are completely satisfactory.

   d. The consonant before the vowel must be different, as in "flight" and "height." Therefore "fare" and "affair" are not satisfactory rhymes.

   e. English is poor in rhymes compared to many other European languages, such as Italian and German. What are called half-rhymes are therefore used even by the most admired poets. Examples are "sun" and "gone," "love" and "move," and "allow" and "bestow." Myself, I do not regard half-rhymes as genuinely legitimate, because they are inevitably noticed when they occur, which is bound to be a distraction from what the poet is trying to get across.

11. Verse which scans but has no rhymes is called *blank verse*, although, strictly speaking, blank verse is any kind of unrhymed verse.

12. The last element of verse-writing that needs a mention is the *stanza*, more popularly called the *verse*. A stanza is an ordered division of verse and can be made up of any number of lines, perhaps most often four. Perhaps the commonest stanza is the four-line one with lines of eight syllables alternating with lines of eight syllables, with the alternate lines rhyming with each other, as in many Church of England hymns.

The selection of the kind of stanza, metrical system and rhyming system for any piece of verse is a matter of considerable importance, requiring careful thought. Different systems produce different emotional effects and moods on the listener and reader, just as in music. The skill at choosing will gradually develop with practice and by examining what poets of the past have done. An example of a perfectly chosen metre is Longfellow's *Song of Hiawatha* ("Listen to this simple story, / To this Song of Hiawatha!"), its effect being of the water of Lake Superior, which is the main setting, rippling in the reader's ears throughout the poem's many verses.

13. As noted in Chapter 9, an important element in the writing of prose is that the *manner* in which the message is conveyed to the reader should be unnoticeable. Drawing attention to the manner of the message will distract attention from the message itself.

In verse, this principle does not apply. One of the reasons for putting something into verse is to make the message more vivid and more easy to remember. What might be called "special effects" are therefore desirable—the more the reader admires and enjoys the manner, the more powerful will be the effect of the message.

Here I shall draw attention to just one much-used special effect, leaving readers to consult textbooks and well-known poetry of the past for others. *Alliteration* is repeating the same sound at the beginning of two or more words. An example is the classic "Round and round the rugged rock the ragged rascal ran."

That is all that I am going to say on the technical side. Now, please, dear readers, get down to some practising—

all of you; no exceptions! Everyone *can* do it, and everyone *should* do it, as I tried to show at the beginning of this chapter.

In your practising:

1. Do *not,* at first, tackle any subjects of any depth or difficulty. At this stage, you should not even consider writing verse on what you most want to write about. Once again, *science* first, *art* second. Technique must come first, and *only* when mastery of technique has been achieved are you ready to move on and develop your *style.*

2. At this stage in learning the skill, it is probably best to aim at making your verses amusing. In the first place, this forces you to avoid the tackling of serious topics that I have labelled as inappropriate at the beginning. In the second place, genuinely amusing verse—in which one has succeeded in avoiding making a fool of oneself in one's efforts to be funny—is more difficult to put together than are any other forms of verse, and once you can manage the more difficult, you are well situated to manage anything easier. In the third place, you are much more likely to know if you have been successful than with any other form of verse. If you submit it for the judgement of others, they will have no difficulty in assessing whether its intended effect has worked with them or is embarrassing.

3. When you have come to the end of your piece of verse, do not stop there. Refine it and refine it and refine it until you believe it to be perfect enough of its kind to need no further refining to improve it. You will find, if you do this conscientiously, that you will gradually need to do this less in future efforts at versifying.

4. This sort of light-hearted verse-writing is recommended only for the purpose of obtaining a thorough mastery of the technique. Once that is achieved, then is the time to use the skill you have learnt in order to write poetry, if you have poetry "in you." The *science* is now available to you for the creation of *art*. And please note and be persuaded of the following:

    a. Traditionally, the purpose of the fine arts, of which poetic literature is of course one, has not been considered to be that of self-indulgence, but that of trying to make the world a better place, in however small a degree.

    b. In practice, this means: that (i) your message must be worth saying and of some benefit to those to whom you wish to communicate it; (ii) it must be expressed with unmistakable clarity (which by no means necessarily means as simply as possible); (iii) what you are trying to do by putting your message into poetic form is to make it more vivid, appealing and memorable.

In bare summary, write poetry for the purpose of *communicating* rather than for the purpose of *expressing yourself*.

Meanwhile, here are some fundamental rules for versification. They are based on some notes that I put together some time ago in the expectation of finding them useful for pupils to whom I might be teaching English at any time in the future.

1. Obviously, the first thing to be selected is the subject. The second is normally the scanning scheme. The third is the rhyming scheme. In practice, scanning schemes and rhyming schemes are probably usually chosen at about the same time.

2. Some verses have *every two lines in succession* scanning the same (couplets). Others have *alternate* lines that scan the same. More complicated scanning schemes are of course possible, even much more complicated ones.

3. The scanning does not only consist of getting the same number of syllables in the lines that are being scanned together. Scanning is done in "feet" of either two syllables or three syllables each. Normally, each "foot" should have the same number of syllables, with the stress in the same place as in the corresponding "foot" in the other line.

4. There should be no false rhythm/scansion—that is, in the "matching" lines, (a) there should be the same number of beats per line, and (b) the stressed syllables should be in the same places.

5. Some verses can have every second line rhyming with its predecessor, others can have every alternate line rhyming, yet others have lines with two or more rhymes inside them. (The American song-writer Cole Porter was notably expert at three-rhyme lines.) And even more complicated rhyming schemes than those are possible. At this stage of trying to acquire mastery, there should be no lines which do not rhyme. For instance, the quite common rhyming—as in many Church of England hymns—of only second and fourth lines, but not the first and third lines—is too "lazy" in appearance for our purpose.

6. There should be no false rhymes such as "tune" with "moon,"* "fleece" with "please," "move" with "shove," or "bother" with "rather" (as in Lerner and Loewe's *My Fair Lady,* as mentioned earlier), let alone "cat" with "mats," or "clever" with "severed" or even "weathered," and let alone, even more so, "clever" with "endeavoured."

7. At the beginning of your practising, take care to choose rhyme-words that it is easy to find matching rhyme-words for, since otherwise you will be making unnecessary difficulties for yourself.

8. As soon as possible, try to think in lines rather than trying to build up your lines word by word. Once

---

* "Tune" and "moon" are always a false rhyme in England, where "tune" is pronounced as if it were written "tewn." In much of America, however, "tune" is pronounced as if it were written "toon," in which case "tune" and "moon" are of course not a false rhyme.

a line has been drafted, *then* try to improve it by changing individual words in it or the order of the words.

9. There should be no rhymes that are so obvious that, after you have read the last word in one line, you are in no doubt what word the writer is going to use to rhyme with it in a subsequent line. In other words the rhyming should always be at least a little unexpected; otherwise the reader will feel let down.

10. There should be a genuine "last line," a sort of climax. Both the sense of the last line and the rhyme at the end of it should be at least a little better than in any of the earlier lines.

11. The verse or poem should always be perfect, even if, in order to achieve this, it is necessary to make it shorter (i.e., reduce the number of scanning and/or rhyming difficulties).

12. Classic light-verse writers whose work can usefully be studied for the purpose of learning from it are W. S. Gilbert of the Gilbert and Sullivan partnership, from whom all his successors learnt, most notably Irving Berlin, Cole Porter and Noël Coward, and whom probably none surpassed.

I close with two examples at opposite extremes of what verse-writing is for. Both examples are well-known compositions.

The first is a piece of verse by W. S. Gilbert which, in

what it sets out to do, could not do it better. Put to music by Sir Arthur Sullivan for the operetta *The Mikado,* it incorporates as many of the features of verse-writing that I have included in this chapter as is likely to be possible in the four lines. Stanza-construction; metre, including at least one each of iambuses, trochees, anapaests, dactyls, amphibrachs and even spondees; perfect rhyming; caesuras occurring in the middle of feet; surely uniquely spectacular alliteration; elegant wit; and much else—it should provide instruction and inspiration for beginners and the more advanced alike. First scan it completely in every respect, and then see if you can do better!

To sit in solemn silence in a dull, dark dock,
In a pestilential prison, with a life-long lock,
Awaiting the sensation of a short, sharp shock,
From a cheap and chippy chopper on a big black block.

Those who end up finding the scanning too difficult are welcome to contact the author of this essay!

My second and last offering is one of the best-known and most influential pieces of poetry in all history. Time was when it was learnt by heart by almost every English schoolboy; and to know its contents thoroughly is a step towards its becoming part of one's character and affecting one's conduct for life.

It is fair to say that, in its technical competence, it could not be improved upon. The author, Rudyard Kipling, was a master of all the many forms of literature that he turned his hand to, and this shows here as clearly as anywhere. Much can be learned by studying how he brings off his effects—for instance, the always faultless scanning, varied and therefore made more appealing by alternate lines having an extra short syllable; the odd-numbered lines ending with an amphibrach and the even-numbered ones with an iambus; the often clever rhyming; the astonishing concept, triumphantly realised, of all thirty-two lines comprising a single sentence; and the superbly worded climax to which the whole poem has been building up.

"If" by Rudyard Kipling, written in 1895 and first published in his book *Rewards and Fairies*.

If you can keep your head when all about you
Are losing theirs and blaming it on you;
If you can trust yourself when all men doubt you,
But make allowance for their doubting too:
If you can wait and not be tired by waiting,
Or being lied about, don't deal in lies,
Or being hated don't give way to hating,
And yet don't look too good, nor talk too wise;

If you can dream—and not make dreams your master;
If you can think—and not make thoughts your aim,
If you can meet with Triumph and Disaster
And treat those two impostors just the same:
If you can bear to hear the truth you've spoken

Twisted by knaves to make a trap for fools,
Or watch the things you gave your life to, broken,
And stoop and build 'em up with worn-out tools;

If you can make one heap of all your winnings
And risk it on one turn of pitch-and-toss,
And lose, and start again at your beginnings
And never breathe a word about your loss:
If you can force your heart and nerve and sinew
To serve your turn long after they are gone,
And so hold on when there is nothing in you
Except the Will which says to them: "Hold on!"

If you can talk with crowds and keep your virtue,
Or walk with Kings—nor lose the common touch,
If neither foes nor loving friends can hurt you,
If all men count with you, but none too much:
If you can fill the unforgiving minute
With sixty seconds' worth of distance run,
Yours is the Earth and everything that's in it,
And—which is more—you'll be a Man, my son!

Against the background of that poem, an especially important point to make is this. It is the *manner* of that message of Kipling's which makes it so memorable and gives it its power, its energy, its penetration and its influence. In prose, however well-written, or in modern, formless so-called verse, the message would be scarcely known and little remembered by the relative few who did come across it. Real poetry, in other words, enables one to say much better—very much better—what is worth saying.

In which context, even though at the cost of momentarily bursting through the confines of what this book is about, I make this final offering. As indicated a few pages back, for most of history, the purpose of writing, as of all art, has been recognised as that of contributing, in however small a way, to making the world a better place. It was not considered to be that of writing about oneself and of self-indulgently exposing one's insides, as is the case with the much modern poetry so-called. I suggest to all my readers, therefore, that, once you have made yourself master of the manner of any message, the technical skills needed to express yourself well in verse, that you pay at least as much attention to choosing worthwhile messages to send forth as to the manner in which you express them.[*]

---

[*] Thomas Hughes, author of another of the most influential pieces of literature of all time, included this in the Preface to the sixth edition of his *Tom Brown's Schooldays:*

"Several persons, for whose judgment I have the highest respect, while saying very kind things about this book, have added, that the great fault of it is 'too much preaching'; but they hope I shall amend in this matter should I ever write again. Now this I most distinctly decline to do. Why, my whole object in writing at all was to get the chance of preaching! When a man comes to my time of life and has his bread to make, and very little time to spare, is it likely that he will spend almost the whole of his yearly vacation in writing a story just to amuse people? I think not. At any rate, I wouldn't do so myself."

PART II

Strunk on Style

Foreword by N. M. Gwynne

What is reproduced here is the 1918 original of *The Elements of Style* with some small adjustments that we can be confident that Strunk would not have objected to. Specifically: I have much improved the way in which it is set out. I have made some small clarifications to reflect the differences between American English and British English. I have added a single paragraph (at the end of number 2 of his Chapter 2) that a development since Strunk's day made desirable, very occasional examples to his examples for greater clarification, and one or two explanations and comments (either indicated by square brackets or in a footnote) when these have seemed necessary. I have also removed a chapter that now serves no evident useful purpose.

In the Preface, I have already said enough to indicate

the quality and even the importance of what now follows. Here, therefore, I shall limit my contribution to this Part II by first outlining exactly what it is that style consists of, together with how best to acquire a style, or indeed a number of styles, that one can justifiably be satisfied with, and then preaching a short sermon both to budding writers and to experienced writers who would like to improve on the competence they have already achieved.

Our style, which can vary from one need to another, is the manner in which we put our sentences together, combine them into paragraphs and combine the paragraphs into whatever they are part of. Style may be good or bad; vigorous or feeble; clear or obscure; plain or ornate; firm and concise or insipid and slipshod; and so on. It reflects our thoughts and our ability to think, and indeed the order and movement we put into our thinking.

The purpose of style, and of studying how to develop it, is so that we can present our thoughts to others in ways that are clear, when necessary forcible, and also graceful.

To develop a good style, what are needed are: (1) clear thinking, without which acquiring good style can hardly start; (2) reading the best writers, and noticing and remembering how they produce their effects; (3) frequent writing, at least at first very much preferably under the supervision of a competent teacher; (4) careful polishing of what we have written. In short, it involves taking *much* trouble, especially in the early early stages, and steadfastly being indifferent to any concern about, or for that matter accusation of, pedantry. Forming the habit of attention to every tiniest detail is very much part of becoming an excellent writer, one who is capable of communicating exactly what is wanted in the most winning way.

All this is so important that it is worth expanding on it.

Most often the word "style" is used to indicate the contrast between the writing of one person and that of another person, or even the writing by one person for one purpose or another purpose. That is not how the word is used in this book. Rather, it is intended to cover what must be learnt by every writer who has acquired an adequate vocabulary and grasp of grammar. As is obvious as soon as it is pointed out, vocabulary and grammar by themselves are not even enough to make writing readable; let alone enough to enable the writer to convey to the reader what he wants to convey in the most readily understandable and convincing way. When putting the message across, the last thing a writer wants is for the reader to be distracted from the message by having to try to puzzle out what the message actually is.[*]

It follows from this that a piece of writing, if it is to do

---

[*] "Life is short, and those who will not take the trouble to write clearly cannot properly expect to be read," was the advice to aspiring academics of Professor Hugh Trevor-Roper, one of the best-known historians and most widely read authors on historical matters of his day. (*One Hundred Letters from Hugh Trevor-Roper,* edited by Richard Davenport-Hines and Adam Sisman [Oxford University Press, 2014], [page number 139]). In other words, when writing a book or article, he regarded its presentation as being as important as the research that went into it.

the job that the writer wants it to do, needs to be much more than technically correct as to its English. It needs also to be well constructed. Specifically . . .

It needs to be divided into paragraphs of suitable length, with each paragraph-break occurring in the most suitable place. The individual paragraphs themselves must be constructed from the building-blocks of the right number of sentences for the purpose, and with each sentence of the right length. In turn, the sentences must be constructed from the building blocks of clauses that are suitable in number, kind and length. And so on. All writers must master these basics methodically before they are ready to build on them in accordance with whatever individual talents they have, and to develop their own individual styles.

Once that is done, *and not before,* and I say this most urgently though by no means exclusively to teachers of young children, the time has at last come for the writer to start being "creative" in the sense that it is understood today. Before then, "creativity" should be discouraged; all too often the result of it would be an accumulation of bad habits.

I offer now my sermon, addressed not only to beginners but even to many experienced writers as well.

Remember always, when you are writing for anyone other than yourself, that you are *giving.* Do not, therefore, write to suit yourself; write with your readers constantly at the forefront of your mind. Put yourself in their shoes when you are deciding how to express yourself. It is not enough that you yourself can easily understand what you are writing down; you are not writing for yourself. Will _they_ understand it? Can you make what you have just written clearer so that there is no possible excuse for their misunderstanding it or even for their having to pause over it for a second or two in order to see its meaning?

If you have made this your ambition, and have taken the first step by mastering the basics of grammar, here now is Professor Strunk to be your matchless guide for the rest of your journey.

CHAPTER 1

Introductory

What follows is intended for use in English courses in which the practice of composition is combined with the study of literature. It aims to give in brief space the principal requirements of plain English style. It covers only a small portion of the field of English style, but the experience of its writer has been that, once past the essentials, students profit most by individual instruction based on the problems of their own work and that each instructor has his own body of theory, which he prefers to that offered by any textbook.

It is an old observation that the best writers sometimes disregard the rules of rhetoric. When they do so, however, the reader will usually find in the sentence some compensating merit, attained at the cost of the violation. Unless he is certain of doing as well, he will probably do best to follow the rules. After he has learnt, by their guidance, to write plain English adequate for everyday uses, let him look, for the secrets of style, to the study of the masters of literature.

Elementary Rules of Usage

1. Form the possessive singular of nouns with 's. Follow this rule whatever the final consonant. Thus write,

> Charles's friend.
> Burns's poems.
> the witch's malice.

This is the usage of the Oxford University Press and of the U.S. Government Printing Office. Exceptions in England are the possessives of ancient proper names ending in "-es" and "-is," the possessive "Jesus'," and such forms as "for conscience' sake" and "for righteousness' sake." They used to be exceptions in America as well, but the more usual rule now is to add 's after the final s in all such instances other than in the "for . . . sake" expressions. Where the old usage is kept, such forms as "Achilles' heel," "Moses' laws" and "Isis' temple" are commonly replaced by

> the heel of Achilles.
> the laws of Moses.
> the temple of Isis.

The pronominal possessives "hers," "its," "theirs," "yours" and "oneself" have no apostrophe.

2. In a series of three or more terms with a single conjunction, in British English the general rule is to use a comma after each term except the one immediately before the conjunction, and in American English the invariable rule is to use a comma after each term.[*] The exceptions in British English are where there is a change of emphasis in the last term or some other reason to suggest to the reader that he should pause briefly when he comes to it. The examples below should make it clear when such exceptions are needed.

Thus write,

> red, white and blue (red, white, and blue in American English).
> honest, energetic, but headstrong.

---

* This is no longer the invariable rule in American English, and I have not followed it in this book.

He opened the letter, read it, and made a note of its
contents.

As noted in number 3 below, the abbreviation "etc.,"
even if only a single term comes before it, is always preceded by a comma. If it is not at the end of a sentence, it
should, logically, be followed by a comma as well. Thus:
"To deride the contents of this book as old-fashioned, out-
of-date, no longer relevant, etc., would be a serious mistake." [Although many, perhaps most, writers would omit
the closing comma there, Strunk and I are united in insisting that it should be included.]

3. **Enclose parenthetic expressions between commas.**
Thus: "The best way to see a country, unless you are
pressed for time, is to travel on foot."

This rule is difficult to apply; it is frequently hard to
decide whether a single word, such as "however," or a brief
phrase, is or is not parenthetic. If the interruption to the
flow of the sentence is but slight, the writer may safely omit
the commas. But whether the interruption be slight or considerable, he must never omit one comma and leave the
other. Such punctuation as "Marjorie's husband, Colonel
Nelson paid us a visit yesterday" or "My brother you will
be pleased to hear, is now in perfect health" is indefensible.

Non-restrictive relative clauses are, in accordance
with this rule, set off by commas. Thus:

> "The audience, which had at first been indifferent,
> became more and more interested."

Similar clauses introduced by "where" and "when" are similarly punctuated. Thus:

> "In 1769, when Napoleon was born, Corsica had but
> recently been acquired by France."
> "Nether Stowey, where Coleridge wrote *The Rime
> of the Ancient Mariner,* is a few miles from
> Bridgwater."

In these sentences, the clauses introduced by "which," "when" and "where" are non-restrictive; they do not limit the application of the words on which they depend, but add, parenthetically, statements supplementing those in the principal clauses. Each sentence is a combination of two statements which might have been made independently. Thus:

> "The audience was at first indifferent. Later it became
> more and more interested."
> "Napoleon was born in 1769. At that time, Corsica had
> but recently been acquired by France."
> "Coleridge wrote *The Rime of the Ancient Mariner* at
> Nether Stowey. Nether Stowey is only a few miles
> from Bridgwater."

Restrictive relative clauses are not set off by commas. Thus:

> "The candidate who best meets these requirements
>   will obtain the place."

In this sentence, the relative clause restricts the application of the word "candidate" to a single person. Unlike those above, the sentence cannot be split into two independent statements.

The abbreviation "etc." is always preceded by a comma and, except at the end of a sentence, followed by one.

Similar in principle to the enclosing of parenthetic expressions between commas is the setting off by commas of phrases or dependent clauses preceding or following the main clause of a sentence. The sentences quoted in this section and under Rules 4, 5, 6, 7, 16 and 18 should afford sufficient guidance.

4. Place a comma before "and" or "but" introducing an independent clause. Thus:

> "The early records of the city have disappeared,
>   and the story of its first years can no longer be
>   reconstructed."
> "The situation is perilous, but there is still one chance
>   of escape."

Sentences of this type, isolated from their context, may seem to be in need of rewriting. As they make complete sense when the comma is reached, the second clause has the appearance of an afterthought. Further, "and" is the least specific of connectives. Used between independent clauses, it indicates only that a relation exists between them without defining that relation. In the example above, the relation is that of cause and result. The two sentences might be rewritten:

"Because the early records of the city have disappeared, the story of its first years can no longer be reconstructed."

"Although the situation is perilous, there is still one chance of escape."

Or the subordinate clauses might be replaced by phrases:

"Owing to the disappearance of the early records of the city, the story of its first years can no longer be reconstructed."

"In this perilous situation, there is still one chance of escape."

But a writer may err by making his sentences too uniformly compact and periodic, and an occasional loose sentence prevents the style from becoming too formal and gives the reader a certain relief. Consequently, loose sentences of the type first quoted are common in easy, unstudied writing. But a writer should be careful not to construct too many of his sentences after this pattern (see Rule 14 in Chapter 3).

Two-part sentences of which the second member is introduced by "as" (in the sense of "because"), "for," "or," "nor," and "while" (in the sense of "at the same time") likewise require a comma before the conjunction.

If a dependent clause, or an introductory phrase requiring to be set off by a comma, precedes the second independent clause, no comma is needed after the conjunction. Thus:

> "The situation is perilous, but if we are prepared to act promptly, there is still one chance of escape."

For two-part sentences connected by an adverb, see the next section.

5. **Do not join independent clauses by a comma.** If two or more clauses, grammatically complete and not joined by a conjunction, are to form a single compound sentence, the proper mark of punctuation is a semicolon.

> "Stevenson's romances are entertaining; they are full of exciting adventures."
> "It is nearly half past five; we cannot reach town before dark."

It is of course equally correct to write the above as two sentences each, replacing the semicolons with periods:

> "Stevenson's romances are entertaining. They are full
>   of exciting adventures."
> "It is nearly half past five. We cannot reach town
>   before dark."

If a conjunction is inserted, the proper mark is a comma (Rule 4).

> "Stevenson's romances are entertaining, for they are
>   full of exciting adventures."
> "It is nearly half past five, and we cannot reach town
>   before dark."

Note that if the second clause is preceded not by a conjunction, but by an adverb, such as "accordingly," "besides," "so," "then," "therefore" or "thus," the semicolon is still required.

> "I had never been in the place before; so I had
>   difficulty in finding my way about."

In general, however, it is best, in writing, to avoid using "so" in this manner; there is danger that the writer who uses it at all may use it too often. A simple correction, usually serviceable, is to omit the word "so," and begin the first clause with "as":

"As I had never been in the place before, I had
    difficulty in finding my way about."

If the clauses are very short, and are alike in form, a comma is usually permissible:

"Man proposes, God disposes."
"The gate swung apart, the bridge fell, the portcullis
    was drawn up."

6. Do not break sentences in two. In other words, do not use periods for commas. Thus:

"I met them on a Cunard liner several years
    ago. Coming home from Liverpool to New
    York."
"He was an interesting talker. A man who had
    travelled all over the world, and lived in half
    a dozen countries."

In both these examples, the first period should be replaced by a comma, and the following word begun with a small letter.

It is permissible to make an emphatic word or expression serve the purpose of a sentence and to punctuate it accordingly:

"Again and again he called out. No reply."

The writer must, however, be certain that the emphasis is warranted and that he will not be suspected of a mere blunder in punctuation.

Rules 3, 4, 5 and 6 cover the most important principles in the punctuation of ordinary sentences; they should be so thoroughly mastered that their application becomes second nature.

7. **A participial phrase at the beginning of a sentence must refer to the grammatical subject.** Thus:

"Walking slowly down the road, he saw a woman accompanied by two children."

The word "walking" refers to the subject of the sentence, not to the woman. If the writer wishes to make it refer to the woman, he must recast the sentence:

"He saw a woman, accompanied by two children, walking slowly down the road."

Participial phrases preceded by a conjunction or by a preposition, nouns in apposition, adjectives, and adjective-phrases come under the same rule if they begin the sentence.

> "On arriving in Chicago, his friends met him at the station" should be: "When he arrived (*or,* On his arrival) in Chicago, his friends met him at the station."
>
> "A soldier of proved valour, they entrusted him with the defence of the city" should be: "A soldier of proved valour, he was entrusted with the defence of the city."
>
> "Young and inexperienced, the task seemed easy to me" should be: "Young and inexperienced, I thought the task easy."
>
> "Without a friend to counsel him, the temptation proved irresistible" should be: "Without a friend to counsel him, he found the temptation irresistible."

Sentences violating this rule are often ludicrous, as here: "Being in a dilapidated condition, I was able to buy the house very cheap."

8. Divide words at line-ends, in accordance with their formation and pronunciation. If there is room at the end of a line for one or more syllables of a word, but not for the whole word, divide the word, unless this involves cutting off only a single letter or cutting off only two letters of a long word. No hard and fast rule for all words can be laid down. The principles most frequently applicable are:

i. **Divide the word according to its formation.** Thus, "know-ledge" (not "knowl-edge"); "Shake-speare" (not "Shakes-peare"); "de-scribe" (not "des-cribe"); "atmo-sphere" (not "atmos-phere").

ii. **Divide "on the vowel":** "edi-ble" (not "ed-ible"); "propo-sition"; "ordi-nary"; "espe-cial"; "reli-gious"; "oppo-nents"; "regu-lar"; "classi-fi-ca-tion" (three different divisions possible); "deco-rative"; "presi-dent."

iii. **Divide between double letters, unless they come at the end of the simple form of the word:** "Apen-nines"; "Cincin-nati"; "refer-ring"; but "tell-ing."

The treatment of consonants in combination is best shown from examples: "for-tune"; "pic-ture"; "presump-tuous"; "illus-tration"; "sub-stan-tial" (either division); "indus-try"; "instruc-tion"; "sug-ges-tion"; "incen-diary."

The student will do well to examine the syllable division in a number of pages of any carefully printed book.

CHAPTER 3

Elementary Principles
of Composition

9. Make the paragraph the unit of composition: one paragraph to each topic. If the subject on which you are writing is of slight extent, or if you intend to treat it very briefly, there may be no need of subdividing it into topics. Thus a brief description, a brief summary of a literary work, a brief account of a single incident, a narrative merely outlining an action, the setting forth of a single idea—any one of these is best written in a single paragraph. After the paragraph has been written, it should be examined to see whether subdivision will not improve it.

Ordinarily, however, a subject requires subdivision into topics, each of which should be made the subject of a paragraph. The object of treating each topic in a paragraph by itself is, of course, to aid the reader. The beginning of each paragraph is a signal to him that a new step in the development of the subject has been reached.

The extent of subdivision will vary with the length of the composition. For example, a short notice of a book or poem might consist of a single paragraph. One slightly longer might consist of two paragraphs:

1. Account of the work.
2. Critical discussion.

A report on a poem, written for a class in literature, might consist of seven paragraphs:

1. Facts of composition and publication.
2. Kind of poem; metrical form.
3. Subject.
4. Treatment of subject.
5. For what the poem is chiefly remarkable.
6. Wherein the poem is characteristic of the writer.
7. The poem's relationship to other works.

The contents of paragraphs 3 and 4 would vary with the poem. Usually, paragraph 3 would indicate the actual or imagined circumstances of the poem (the situation), if these call for explanation, and would then state the subject and outline its development. If the poem is a narrative in the third person throughout, paragraph 3 need contain no more than a concise summary of the action. Paragraph 4 would indicate the leading ideas and show how they are made prominent or would indicate what points in the narrative are chiefly emphasised.

A novel might be discussed under the following heads:

1. Setting.
2. Plot.
3. Characters.
4. Purpose.

A historical event might be discussed under the heads:

1. What led up to the event.
2. Account of the event.
3. What the event led up to.

In treating either of these last two subjects, the writer would probably find it necessary to subdivide one or more of the topics here given.

As a rule, single sentences should not be written or printed as paragraphs. An exception may be made of sentences of transition, indicating the relation between the parts of an exposition or argument.

In dialogue, each speech, even if only a single word, is a paragraph by itself; that is, a new paragraph begins with each change of speaker. The application of this rule, when dialogue and narrative are combined, is best learnt from examples in well-printed works of fiction.

10. **As a rule, begin each paragraph with a topic sentence; end it in conformity with the beginning.** Again, the object is to aid the reader. The practice here recommended enables him to discover the purpose of each paragraph as he begins to read it and to retain the purpose in mind as he ends it. For this reason, the most generally useful kind of paragraph, particularly in exposition and argument, is that in which

1. the topic sentence comes at or near the beginning;
2. the succeeding sentences explain or establish or develop the statement made in the topic sentence; and
3. the final sentence either emphasises the thought of the topic sentence or states some important consequence.

Ending with a digression, or with an unimportant detail, is particularly to be avoided.

If the paragraph forms part of a larger composition, its relation to what precedes, or its function as a part of the whole, may need to be expressed. This can sometimes be done by a mere word or phrase—"again"; "therefore"; "for the same reason"—in the topic sentence. Sometimes, however, it is expedient to precede the topic sentence by one or more sentences of introduction or transition. If more than one such sentence is required, it is generally better to set apart the transitional sentences as a separate paragraph.

According to the writer's purpose, he may, as indicated above, relate the body of the paragraph to the topic sentence in one or more of several different ways. He may make the meaning of the topic sentence clearer by restating it in other forms, by defining its terms, by denying the converse, by giving illustrations or specific instances; he may establish it by proofs; or he may develop it by showing its implications and consequences. In a long paragraph, he may carry out several of these processes.

1. "Now, to be properly enjoyed, a walking tour should be gone upon alone." (One-topic sentence.)

2. "If you go in a company, or even in pairs, it is no longer a walking tour in anything but name; it is something else and more in the nature of a picnic." (The meaning has been made clearer by denial of the contrary.)

3. "A walking tour should be gone upon alone, because freedom is of the essence; because you should be able to stop and go on, and follow this way or that, as the freak takes you; and because you must have your own pace, and neither trot alongside a champion walker, nor mince in time with a girl." (The topic sentence has been repeated, in abridged

form, and supported by three reasons; the meaning of the third—"you must have your own pace"— made clearer by denying the converse.)

4. "And you must be open to all impressions and let your thoughts take colour from what you see." (A fourth reason has been given, stated in two forms.)

5. "You should be as a pipe for any wind to play upon." (The same reason again, stated in still another form.)

6. "I cannot see the wit," says Hazlitt, "of walking and talking at the same time. When I am in the country, I wish to vegetate like the country, which is the gist of all that can be said upon the matter." (The same reason yet again, this time as stated by Hazlitt.)

7. "There should be no cackle of voices at your elbow, to jar on the meditative silence of the morning." (Repetition, in paraphrase, of the quotation from Hazlitt.)

8. "And so long as a man is reasoning he cannot surrender himself to that fine intoxication that comes of much motion in the open air, that begins in a sort of dazzle and sluggishness of the brain, and ends in a peace that passes comprehension." —Stevenson, *Walking Tours*. (Final statement of the fourth reason, in language amplified and heightened to form a strong conclusion.)

Further examples:

1. "It was chiefly in the eighteenth century that a very different conception of history grew up." (One-topic sentence.)

2. "Historians then came to believe that their task was not so much to paint a picture as to solve a problem; to explain or illustrate the successive phases of national growth, prosperity, and adversity." (The meaning of the topic sentence is made clearer; the new conception of history defined.)

3. "The history of morals, of industry, of intellect, and of art; the changes that take place in manners or beliefs; the dominant ideas that prevailed in successive periods; the rise, fall, and modification of political constitutions; in a word, all the conditions of national well-being became the subjects of their works." (The definition has been expanded.)

4. "They sought rather to write a history of peoples than a history of kings." (The definition is now explained by contrast.)

5. "They looked especially in history for the chain of causes and effects." (The definition is supplemented: another element in the new conception of history.)

6. "They undertook to study in the past the physiology of nations, and hoped by applying the experimental method on a large scale to deduce some lessons of real value about the conditions on which the

welfare of society mainly depend." —Lecky, *The Political Value of History*. (Conclusion: an important consequence of the new conception of history.)

In narration and description, the paragraph sometimes begins with a concise, comprehensive statement serving to hold together the details that follow. Thus:

"The breeze served us admirably."
"The campaign opened with a series of reverses."
"The next ten or twelve pages were filled with a curious set of entries."

But this device, if too often used, would become a mannerism. More commonly, the opening sentence simply indicates by its subject with what the paragraph is to be principally concerned.

"At length I thought I might return towards the stockade."
"He picked up the heavy lamp from the table and began to explore."
"Another flight of steps, and they emerged on the roof."

The brief paragraphs of animated narrative, however, are often without even this semblance of a topic sentence. The break between them serves the purpose of a rhetorical pause, throwing into prominence some detail of the action.

11. **Tend to use the active voice.** The active voice is usually more direct and vigorous than the passive:

> "I shall always remember my first visit to Boston" is much better than: "My first visit to Boston will always be remembered by me."

The latter sentence is less direct, less bold and less concise. If the writer tries to make it more concise by omitting "by me," as in "My first visit to Boston will always be remembered," it becomes indefinite. Is it the writer, or some person undisclosed, or the world at large, that will always remember this visit?

This general rule does not, of course, mean that the writer should entirely discard the passive voice, which is frequently convenient and sometimes necessary. Thus, in "The dramatists of the Restoration are little esteemed today" and "Modern readers have little esteem for the dramatists of the Restoration," the first would be the right form in a paragraph on the dramatists of the Restoration; the second, in a paragraph on the tastes of modern readers. The need of making a particular word the subject of the sentence will often, as in these examples, determine which voice is to be used.

The habitual use of the active voice, however, makes for forcible writing. This is true not only in narrative principally concerned with action but in writing of any kind. Many a tame sentence of description or exposition can be made lively and emphatic by substituting a transitive in the active voice for some such perfunctory expression as "there is" or "could be heard."

Thus:

"There was a great number of dead leaves lying on the ground" is improved by "Dead leaves covered the ground."

"The sound of the falls could still be heard" is improved by "The sound of the falls still reached our ears."

"The reason that he left college was that his health had become impaired" is improved by "Failing health compelled him to leave college."

"It was not long before he was very sorry that he had said what he had" is improved by "He soon repented of his words."

As a rule, avoid making one passive depend directly upon another, as in:

"Gold was not allowed to be exported." Rather: "It was forbidden to export gold," or "The export of gold was prohibited."

"He has been proved to have been seen entering the building." Rather: "It has been proved that he was seen to enter the building."

In both the examples above, before correction, the word properly related to the second passive is made the subject of the first.

A common fault is to use, as the subject of a passive construction, a noun which expresses the entire action, leaving to the verb no function beyond that of completing the sentence. Thus:

"A survey of this region was made in 1900" should be "This region was surveyed in 1900."

"Mobilisation of the army was rapidly carried out" should be "The army was rapidly mobilised."

"Confirmation of these reports cannot be obtained" should be "These reports cannot be confirmed."

Compare the sentence "The export of gold was prohibited," in which the predicate "was prohibited" expresses something not implied in "export."

12. Put statements in positive form. Make definite assertions. Avoid tame, colourless, hesitating, non-committal language. Use the word "not" as a means of denial or in antithesis, never as a means of evasion. Thus:

"He was not very often on time." Rather: "He usually came late."

"He did not think that studying Latin was much use."

Rather: "He thought the study of Latin useless."

"*The Taming of the Shrew* is rather weak in spots."

Perhaps rather: "Shakespeare does not portray Katharina as a very admirable character, nor does Bianca remain long in memory as an important character in Shakespeare's works. The women in *The Taming of the Shrew* are unattractive. Katharina is disagreeable, Bianca insignificant."

The last example, before correction, is indefinite as well as negative. The corrected version, consequently, is simply a guess at the writer's intention.

All three examples show the weakness inherent in the word "not." Consciously or unconsciously, the reader is dissatisfied with being told only what is not; he wishes to be told what *is*. Hence, as a rule, it is better to express a negative in positive form. Thus, "not honest" is improved as "dishonest"; "not important" is improved as "trifling"; "did not remember" is improved as "forgot"; "did not pay any attention to" is improved as "ignored"; and "did not have much confidence in" is improved as "distrusted."

The antithesis of negative and positive is strong:

"Not charity, but simple justice."

"Not that I loved Caesar less, but that I loved Rome more."

Negative words other than "not" are usually stronger: "The sun never sets upon the British flag."

13. Omit needless words. Vigorous writing is *concise*. A sentence should contain no unnecessary words, a paragraph no unnecessary sentences, for the same reason that a drawing should have no unnecessary lines and a machine no unnecessary parts. This requires not that the writer make all his sentences short, or that he avoid all detail and treat his subjects only in outline, but that every word tell.

Many expressions in common use violate this principle:

"the question as to whether" is better as "whether" or "the question whether."

"there is no doubt but that" is better as "no doubt" or "doubtless."

"used for fuel purposes" is better as "used for fuel."

"he is a man who" is better as "he."

"in a hasty manner" is better as "hastily."

"this is a subject which" is better as "this subject."

"His story is a strange one" is better as "His story is strange."

Especially the expression "the fact that" should be revised out of every sentence in which it occurs. Thus:

"owing to the fact that" should be replaced by "since" or "because."

> "in spite of the fact that" should be replaced by "though" or "although."
>
> "call your attention to the fact that" should be replaced by "remind you" or "notify you."
>
> "I was unaware of the fact that" should be replaced by "I was unaware that" or "I did not know."
>
> "the fact that he had not succeeded" should be replaced by "his failure."
>
> "the fact that I had arrived" should be replaced by "my arrival."

See also under "case," "character," "nature" and "system" in Chapter 5.

"Who is," "which was," and the like are often superfluous. Thus:

> Better than "His brother, who is a member of the same firm," is "His brother, a member of the same firm."
>
> Better than "Trafalgar, which was Nelson's last battle," is "Trafalgar, Nelson's last battle."

A positive statement is more concise than a negative statement, and the active voice more concise than the passive voice. Many of the examples given under Rules 11 and 12 illustrate this rule as well.

A common violation of conciseness is the presentation of a single complex idea, step-by-step, in a series of sentences which might to advantage be combined into one.

The following passage has six sentences comprising fifty-one words: "Macbeth was very ambitious. This led him to wish to become king of Scotland. The witches told him that this wish of his would come true. The king of Scotland at this time was Duncan. Encouraged by his wife, Macbeth murdered Duncan. He was thus enabled to succeed Duncan as king."

Nothing is lost and much gained by putting what is conveyed there into a single sentence of twenty-six words: "Encouraged by his wife, Macbeth achieved his ambition and realised the prediction of the witches by murdering Duncan and becoming king of Scotland in his place."

14. **Avoid a succession of loose sentences.** This rule refers especially to loose sentences of a particular type: those consisting of two coordinate clauses, the second introduced by a conjunction or relative. Although single sentences of this type may be unexceptionable (see under Rule 4), a series soon becomes monotonous and tedious.

An unskilful writer will sometimes construct a whole paragraph of sentences of this kind, using as connectives "and," "but" and, less frequently, "who," "which," "when," "where" and "while," these last in non-restrictive senses (see under Rule 3). Take this paragraph:

The third concert of the subscription series was given last evening, and a large audience was in attendance. Mr. Edward Appleton was the soloist, and the Boston Symphony Orchestra furnished the instrumental music. The former showed himself to be an artist of the first rank, while the latter proved itself fully deserving of its high reputation. The interest aroused by the series has been very gratifying to the Committee, and it is planned to give a similar series annually hereafter. The fourth concert will be given on Tuesday, 10 May, when an equally attractive programme will be presented.

Apart from its triteness and emptiness, that paragraph is bad because of the structure of its sentences, with their mechanical symmetry and singsong. Contrast with them the sentences in the paragraphs quoted under Rule 10, or in any piece of good English prose, such as the Preface ("Before the Curtain") to *Vanity Fair.*

If the writer finds that he has written a series of sentences of the type described, he should recast enough of them to remove the monotony, replacing them by simple sentences, by sentences of two clauses joined by a semicolon, by periodic sentences of two clauses, by sentences, loose or periodic, of three clauses—whichever best represent the real relations of the thought.

15. Express coordinate ideas in similar form. This principle, that of parallel construction, requires that expressions of similar content and function be outwardly similar.

The likeness of form enables the reader to recognise more readily the likeness of content and function.

Familiar instances from the Bible are the Ten Commandments, the Beatitudes, and the petitions of "Our Father" Prayer.

The unskilful writer often violates this principle, from a mistaken belief that he should constantly vary the form of his expressions. It is true that in repeating a statement in order to emphasise it, he may have need to vary its form. For illustration, see the paragraph from Stevenson quoted under Rule 10. But apart from this, he should follow the principle of parallel construction.

> "Formerly, science was taught by the textbook method, while now the laboratory method is employed," is improved as "Formerly, science was taught by the textbook method; now it is taught by the laboratory method."

The first version gives the impression that the writer is undecided or timid; he seems unable or afraid to choose one form of expression and hold to it. The second version shows that the writer has at least made his choice and abided by it.

By this principle, an article or a preposition applying to all the members of a series must either be used only before the first term or else be repeated before each term.

"The French, the Italians, Spanish, and Portuguese"
should be "The French, the Italians, the Spanish,
and the Portuguese."

"In spring, summer, or in winter" should be "In spring,
summer, or winter" or "In spring, in summer, or in
winter."

Correlative expressions ("both . . . and"; "not . . . but";
"not only . . . but also"; "either . . . or"; "first, . . . second, . . .
third"; and the like) should be followed by the same grammatical construction. Many violations of this rule can be
corrected by rearranging the sentence.

"It was both a long ceremony and very tedious"
is better as "The ceremony was both long and
tedious."

"A time not for words but action" is better as "A time
not for words but for action."

"Either you must grant his request or incur his ill will"
is better as "You must either grant his request or
incur his ill will."

"My objections are, first, the injustice of the measure;
second, that it is unconstitutional," is better as "My
objections are, first, that the measure is unjust;
second, that it is unconstitutional."

It may be asked: what if a writer needs to express a
very large number of similar ideas, say twenty? Must he

write twenty consecutive sentences of the same pattern? On closer examination he will probably find that the difficulty is imaginary, that his twenty ideas can be classified in groups, and that he need apply the principle only within each group. Otherwise he had best avoid the difficulty by putting his statements in the form of a table.

16. Keep related words together. The position of the words in a sentence is the principal means of showing their relationship. The writer must therefore, so far as possible, bring together the words, and groups of words, that are related in thought and keep apart those which are not so related.

The subject of a sentence and the principal verb should not, as a rule, be separated by a phrase or clause that can be transferred to the beginning. Thus:

> "Wordsworth, in the fifth book of *The Excursion,* gives a minute description of this church" is better as "In the fifth book of *The Excursion,* Wordsworth gives a minute description of this church."
> "Cast iron, when treated in a Bessemer converter, is changed into steel" is better as "By treatment in a Bessemer converter, cast iron is changed into steel."

The objection is that the interposed phrase or clause needlessly interrupts the natural order of the main clause. This objection, however, does not usually hold when the order is interrupted only by a relative clause or by an expression in apposition. Nor does it hold in periodic sentences in which the interruption is a deliberately used means of creating suspense (see examples under Rule 18).

The relative pronoun should come, as a rule, immediately after its antecedent. Therefore,

"There was a look in his eye that boded mischief" is better as "In his eye was a look that boded mischief."

"He wrote three articles about his adventures in Spain, which were published in *Harper's Magazine,*" is better as "He published three articles in *Harper's Magazine* about his adventures in Spain."

"This is a portrait of Benjamin Harrison, grandson of William Henry Harrison, who became president in 1889," is better as "This is a portrait of Benjamin Harrison, grandson of William Henry Harrison. He became president in 1889."

If the antecedent consists of a group of words, the relative comes at the end of the group, unless this would cause ambiguity. Thus:

"The Superintendent of the Chicago Division, who . . ." is correct. But "A proposal to amend the Sherman Act, which has been variously judged" needs to be changed to "A proposal, which has been

variously judged, to amend the Sherman Act"
or "A proposal to amend the much-debated
Sherman Act." And "The grandson of William
Henry Harrison, who . . ." needs to be changed
to "William Henry Harrison's grandson,
Benjamin Harrison, who . . ."

A noun in apposition may come between antecedent and relative, because in such a combination no real ambiguity can arise. This, therefore, does not need to be changed:

"The Duke of York, his brother, who was regarded
with hostility by the Whigs . . ."

Modifiers should come, if possible, next to the word they modify. If several expressions modify the same word, they should be so arranged that no wrong relation is suggested. Thus:

"All the members were not present" should be "Not all
the members were present."
"He only found two mistakes" should be "He found
only two mistakes."
"Major R. E. Joyce will give a lecture on Tuesday
evening in Bailey Hall, to which the public is
invited, titled 'My Experiences in Mesopotamia'
at 8:00 p.m." should be "On Tuesday evening
at 8:00 p.m., Major R. E. Joyce will give a

lecture in Bailey Hall titled 'My Experiences in Mesopotamia.' The public is invited."

17. In summaries, keep to one tense. In summarising the action of a drama, the writer should always use the present tense. In summarising a poem, story, or novel, he should preferably use the present, though he may use the past if he prefers. If the summary is in the present tense, antecedent action should be expressed by the perfect; if in the past, by the past perfect, as in this passage:

> An unforeseen chance prevents Friar John from delivering Friar Lawrence's letter to Romeo. Juliet, meanwhile, owing to her father's arbitrary change of the day set for her wedding, has been compelled to drink the potion on Tuesday night, with the result that Balthasar informs Romeo of her supposed death before Friar Lawrence learns of the non-delivery of the letter.

But whichever tense is used in the summary, a past tense in indirect discourse or in indirect question remains unchanged, as in

> "The Legate inquires who struck the blow."

Apart from the exceptions noted, whichever tense the writer chooses, he should use throughout. Shifting from one tense to the other gives the appearance of uncertainty and irresolution (compare Rule 15).

In presenting the statements or the thought of someone else, as in summarising an essay or reporting a speech, the writer should avoid intercalating such expressions as "he said," "he stated," "the speaker added," "the speaker then went on to say," "the author also thinks," or the like. He should indicate clearly at the outset, once for all, that what follows is summary, and then waste no words in repeating the notification.

In notebooks, in newspapers, in handbooks of literature, summaries of one kind or another may be indispensable, and for children in primary schools it is a useful exercise to retell a story in their own words. But in the criticism or interpretation of literature, the writer should be careful to avoid dropping into summary. He may find it necessary to devote one or two sentences to indicating the subject, or the opening situation, of the work he is discussing; he may cite numerous details to illustrate its qualities. But he should aim to write an orderly discussion supported by evidence, not a summary with occasional comment. Similarly, if the scope of his discussion includes a number of works, he will as a rule do better not to take them up singly in chronological order but to aim from the beginning at establishing general conclusions.

18. Place the emphatic words of a sentence at the end. The proper place for the word, or group of words, that the

writer desires to make most prominent is usually the end of the sentence. Thus:

> "Humanity has hardly advanced in fortitude since that time, though it has advanced in many other ways," is better as "Humanity, since that time, has advanced in many other ways, but it has hardly advanced in fortitude."
>
> "This steel is principally used for making razors because of its hardness," is better as "Because of its hardness, this steel is principally used in making razors."

The word or group of words entitled to this position of prominence is usually the logical predicate—that is, the new element in the sentence—as it is in the second example above.

The effectiveness of the periodic sentence arises from the prominence that it gives to the main statement. Examples:

> "Four centuries ago, Christopher Columbus, one of the Italian mariners whom the decline of their own republics had put at the service of the world and of adventure, seeking for Spain a westward passage to the Indies as a set-off against the achievements of Portuguese discoverers, lighted on America."
>
> "With these hopes and in this belief I would urge

you, laying aside all hindrance, thrusting away all private aims, to devote yourselves unswervingly and unflinchingly to the vigorous and successful prosecution of this war."

The other prominent position in the sentence is the beginning. Any element in the sentence, other than the subject, becomes emphatic when placed first. Examples:

"Deceit or treachery he could never forgive."
"So vast and rude, fretted by the action of nearly three thousand years, the fragments of this architecture may often seem, at first sight, like works of nature."

A subject coming first in its sentence may be emphatic, but hardly by its position alone. In the sentence "Great kings worshipped at his shrine," the emphasis upon "kings" arises largely from its meaning and from the context. To receive special emphasis, the subject of a sentence must take the position of the predicate. For example: "Through the middle of the valley flowed a winding stream."

The principle that the proper place for what is to be made most prominent is the end applies equally to the words of a sentence, to the sentences of a paragraph, and to the paragraphs of a composition.

CHAPTER 4

A Few Matters of Form

Headings. Leave a blank line, or its equivalent in space, after the title or heading of a manuscript. On succeeding pages, if using ruled paper, begin on the first line.

Numerals. Do not spell out dates or other serial numbers. Write them in figures or in Roman notation, as may be appropriate. Thus:

9th August 1918. [Illogically, because logically the order would be shortest, second shortest, third shortest of the three elements of time listed in any date, it has long been "August 9, 1918" in America, a usage which has infected British usage during the last two or three decades.]

Chapter XII.
Rule 3.
352nd Infantry.

Parentheses. A sentence containing an expression in parenthesis is punctuated, outside the marks of parenthesis, exactly as if the expression in parenthesis were absent. The expression within is punctuated as if it stood by itself, except that the final stop is omitted unless it is a question mark or an exclamation mark. Examples:

> "I went to his house yesterday (my third attempt to see him), but he had left town."
> "He declares (and why should we doubt his good faith?) that he is now certain of success."

[When a wholly detached expression or sentence is parenthesised, the final stop comes before the last mark of parenthesis; in other words, inside the bracket which closes it—as in this wholly detached sentence inside a parenthesis.]

Quotations. Formal quotations, cited as documentary evidence, are introduced by a colon and enclosed in quotation marks. Thus:

> "The provision of the Constitution is: 'No Tax or Duty shall be laid on Articles exported from any State.'"

Quotations grammatically in apposition or the direct objects of verbs are preceded by a comma and enclosed in quotation marks. Thus:

"I recall a maxim of La Rochefoucauld's, 'Gratitude is
a lively sense of benefits to come.'"
"Aristotle says, 'Art is an imitation of nature.'"

Quotations introduced by "that" are regarded as being in indirect discourse and not enclosed in quotation marks. Thus:

"Keats declares that beauty is truth, truth beauty."

Proverbial expressions and familiar phrases of literary origin require no quotation marks. Thus:

These are the times that try men's souls.
He lives far from the madding crowd.

The same is true of colloquialisms and slang.

References. In scholarly work requiring exact references, abbreviate titles that occur frequently, giving the full forms in an alphabetical list at the end. As a general practice, give the references in parenthesis or in footnotes, not in the body of the sentence. Omit the words "act," "scene," "line," "book," "volume," "page," except when referring to only one of them. Punctuate as indicated below.

Thus "In the second scene of the third act" should be shown as "In III, ii." Still better, simply insert "III, ii" in parenthesis at the proper place in the sentence.

Other examples:

> "After the killing of Polonius, Hamlet is placed under guard (IV, ii, 14)."
> "2 Samuel 1:17–27."
> "*Othello,* II, iii, 264–267; III, iii, 155–161."

Titles. For the titles of literary works, scholarly usage prefers italics with capitalised initials. The usage of editors and publishers varies, some using italics with capitalised initials, others using Roman with capitalised initials and with or without quotation marks. Use italics (indicated in manuscript by underscoring), except in writing for a periodical that follows a different practice. Thus, *The Iliad. The Odyssey. As You Like It. A Tale of Two Cities.*

CHAPTER 5

Words and Expressions Commonly Misused

Many of the words and expressions here listed are not so much bad English as bad style, the commonplaces of careless writing. As illustrated under Feature, the proper correction is likely to be not the replacement of one word or set of words by another but the replacement of vague generality by definite statement.

All right. Idiomatic in familiar speech as a detached phrase in the sense "Agreed" or "Go ahead." In other uses better avoided. Always written as two words.

As good as or **better than.** Expressions of this type should be corrected by rearranging the sentence. For instance, "My opinion is as good as his, or better" or ". . . if not better."

As to whether. "Whether" is sufficient; see under Rule 13 in Chapter 3.

Bid. Takes the infinitive without "to." The past tense is "bade." Thus "He bade me come"; not "He bade me to come."

Case. The *Concise Oxford Dictionary* begins its definition of this word: "Instance of a thing's occurring; usual state of affairs." In these two senses, the word "case" is usually unnecessary. Thus:

> "In many cases, the rooms were poorly ventilated" should be "Many of the rooms were poorly ventilated."
>
> "It has rarely been the case that any mistake has been made" is better as "Few mistakes have been made."

Certainly. Used indiscriminately by some speakers, much as others use "very," to intensify any and every statement. A mannerism of this kind, bad in speech, is even worse in writing.

Character. Often simply redundant, used from a mere habit of wordiness. "Acts of a hostile character" should be simply "Hostile acts."

Claim, verb. With object-noun, means "lay claim to." May be used with a dependent clause if this sense is clearly involved: "He claimed that he was the sole surviving heir." (But even here, "claimed to be" would be better.) Not to be used as a substitute for "declare," "maintain" or "charge."

Compare. "To compare *to*" is to point out resemblances, or imply resemblances, between objects regarded as essentially of a different order. "To compare *with*" is mainly to point out differences between objects regarded as essentially of the same order. Thus life has been compared *to* a pilgrimage, *to* a drama, *to* a battle; Congress may be compared *with* the British Parliament. Paris has been compared *to* ancient Athens; it may be compared *with* modern London.

Clever. This word has been greatly overused; it is best restricted to ingenuity displayed in small matters.

Consider. Not followed by "as" when it means "believe to be," as in "I consider him thoroughly competent." Compare "The lecturer considered Cromwell first as soldier and second as administrator," where "considered" means "examined" or "discussed."

Dependable. A needless substitute for "reliable," "trustworthy."

Due to. Incorrectly used for "through," "because of," or "owing to" in adverbial phrases such as "He lost the first game due to carelessness." In its correct use, it is related to a particular noun as predicate or as modifier, as in "This invention is due to Edison"; "losses due to preventable fires."

Effect. As a noun, it means "result"; as a verb, it means

"to bring about," "accomplish" (not to be confused with "affect," which means "to influence"). Again as a noun, it is also often loosely used in perfunctory writing about fashions, music, painting, and other arts, as in: "an Oriental effect"; "effects in pale green"; "very delicate effects"; "broad effects"; "subtle effects"; "a charming effect was produced by." The writer who has a definite meaning to express will not take refuge in such vagueness.

Etc. Not to be used of persons. It is equivalent to "and the rest," "and so forth," and hence it is not to be used if one of these would be insufficient—that is, if the reader would be left in doubt as to any important particulars. It is least open to objection when it represents the last terms of a list already given almost in full or immaterial words at the end of a quotation. At the end of a list introduced by "such as," "for example," or any similar expression, "etc." is incorrect.

Fact. Use this word only of matters of a kind capable of direct verification, not of matters of judgement. That a particular event happened on a given date, that lead melts at a certain temperature, are facts. But such conclusions as that Napoleon was the greatest of modern generals, or that the climate of California is delightful, however incontestable they may be, are not properly facts. On the formula "the fact that," see under Rule 13 in Chapter 3.

Factor. A hackneyed word; the expressions of which it forms part can usually be replaced by something more direct and idiomatic. Thus:

"His superior training was the great factor in his winning the match" is better as "He won the match by being better trained."

"Heavy artillery is becoming an increasingly important factor in deciding battles" is better as "Heavy artillery is playing a larger and larger part in deciding battles."

Feature. Another hackneyed word; like "factor," it usually adds nothing to the sentence in which it occurs. Thus instead of "A feature of the entertainment especially worthy of mention was the singing of Miss A.," it is better to use the same number of words to tell what Miss A. sang or, if the programme has already been given, to tell something of *how* she sang. As a verb, in the advertising sense of offer as a special attraction, "to feature" should be avoided.

Fix. Colloquial in America for "arrange," "prepare," "mend." In writing, restrict it to its literary senses: fasten, make firm or immovable, etc.

He is a man who. A common type of redundant expression; see Rule 13 in Chapter 3. "He is a man who is very ambitious" should simply be "He is very ambitious," and "Spain is a country which I have always wanted to visit" should be "I have always wanted to visit Spain."

However. In the meaning "nevertheless," it should not come first in its sentence or clause. Incorrect is: "The roads were almost impassable. However, we at last succeeded in reaching camp." Correct is: "The roads were almost impassable. At last, however, we succeeded in reaching camp." When "however" comes first, it means "in whatever way" or "to whatever extent." Examples: "However you advise him, he will probably do as he thinks best." "However discouraging the prospect, he never lost heart."

Kind of. Not to be used as a substitute for "rather" (before adjectives and verbs), or, except in familiar style, for "something like" (before nouns). Restrict it to its literal sense: "Amber is a kind of fossil resin"; "I dislike that kind of notoriety." The same holds true of "sort of."

Less. Should not be misused for "fewer." Therefore "He had less men than in the previous campaign" should be "He had fewer men than in the previous campaign." "Less" refers to *quantity,* "fewer" to *number.* "His troubles are less than mine" means "His troubles are not so great as mine." "His troubles are fewer than mine" means "His troubles are not so numerous as mine."[*] It is, however, correct to say, "The signers of the petition were less than a hundred," where the round number, a hundred, is something like a collective noun, and "less" is thought of as meaning "a less quantity or amount."

---

* Contrary to what some grammarians would say, Strunk is not incorrect in his use of "so . . . as" rather than "as . . . as" in this instance. As the *Concise Oxford Dictionary* confirms, "so" to express degree before an "as" clause may not be used when making a positive statement, but only with a negative. Thus: "I am not so eager as you" is correct, but "I am so eager as you" is incorrect and should be "I am as eager as you."

Line, *or* along these lines. "Line" in the sense of "course of procedure, conduct, thought" is allowable but has been so much overworked, particularly in the phrase "along these lines," that a writer who aims at freshness or originality had better discard it entirely. Thus:

Better than "Mr. B. also spoke along the same lines" is "Mr. B. also spoke, to the same effect."

Better than "He is studying along the line of French literature" is "He is studying French literature."

Literal, literally. Often incorrectly used in support of exaggeration or violent metaphor, as in:

"A literal flood of abuse" rather than "A flood of abuse."
"Literally dead with fatigue" rather than "Almost dead with fatigue" or "Dead tired."
"He literally looked daggers at me" rather than "He looked daggers at me."

Lose out. Meant to be more emphatic than "lose," but is actually less so because of its commonness. The same holds true of "try out," "win out," "sign up," "register up." With a number of verbs, "out" and "up" form idiomatic combinations: "find out," "run out," "turn out," "cheer up," "dry up," "make up," and others, each distinguishable in meaning from the simple verb. "Lose out" is not in that category.

Most. Not to be used for "almost." Therefore "Most everybody" should be "Almost everybody" and "Most all the time" should be "Almost all the time."

Nature. Often simply redundant, used like "character," as in "Acts of a hostile nature," which should be "Hostile acts." It is often vaguely used in such expressions as "a lover of nature," "poems about nature." Unless more specific statements follow, the reader cannot tell whether the poems have to do with natural scenery, rural life, the sunset, the untracked wilderness, or the habits of squirrels.

Near by. An adverbial phrase, not yet fully accepted as good English, though the analogy of "close by" and "hard by" seems to justify it. "Near," or "near at hand," is as good, if not better. It is not to be used as an adjective. Use "neighbouring" instead. [Since Strunk's day, it has become permissible to compress "near by" into "nearby," when it can be used both as an adverb ("I am staying nearby") and as an adjective ("I am staying in a nearby house").]

Oftentimes. An archaic form, no longer in good use. The modern word is "often."

One hundred and one. Retain the "and" in this and similar expressions, in accordance with the unvarying usage of English prose from Old English times.

One of the most. Avoid beginning essays or paragraphs with this formula, as in "One of the most interesting developments of modern science is, etc." and "Switzerland is one of the most interesting countries of Europe." There is nothing wrong in this; it is simply threadbare and forcible-feeble.

People. "The people" is a political term, not to be confused with "the public." From the people comes political support or opposition; from the public comes artistic appreciation or commercial patronage. The word "people" is not to be used with words of number, in place of "persons." If of "six people" five went away, how many "people" would be left?

Phase. Means a stage of transition or development, as in "the phases of the moon" and "the last phase." It is not to be used for "aspect" or "topic." Thus, "Another phase of the subject" should be "Another point . . ." or "Another question."

Possess. Not to be used as a mere substitute for "have" or "own." Thus:

"He possessed great courage" should be "He had great courage" or "He was very brave."

"He was the fortunate possessor of" should be "He owned."

Respective, respectively. These words may usually be omitted with advantage. Thus:

"Works of fiction are listed under the names of their respective authors" should be "Works of fiction are listed under the names of their authors."

"The one-mile and two-mile runs were won by Jones and Cummings respectively" should be "The one-mile and two-mile runs were won by Jones and by Cummings."

In some kinds of formal writing, as in geometrical proofs, it may be necessary to use "respectively," but it should not appear in writing on ordinary subjects.

So. Avoid, in writing, the use of "so" as an intensifier: "so good"; "so warm"; "so delightful." On the use of "so" to introduce clauses, see Rule 5.

Sort of. See under Kind of.

State. Not to be used as a mere substitute for "say," "remark." Restrict it to the sense of "express fully" or ". . . clearly," as in "He refused to state his objections."

Student body. A needless and awkward expression, meaning no more than the simple word "students." Thus:

"A member of the student body" should be "A student."

"Popular with the student body" should be "Liked by the students."

"The student body passed resolutions" should be "The students passed resolutions."

System. Frequently used without need. Thus:

"Dayton has adopted the commission system of government" is better as "Dayton has adopted government by commission."

"The dormitory system" is better as simply "Dormitories."

Thanking you in advance. This sounds as if the writer meant "It will not be worth my while to write to you again." Simply write "Thanking you." And if the favour that you have requested is granted, write a letter of acknowledgement.

They. A common inaccuracy is the use of the plural pronoun when the antecedent is a distributive expression such as "each," "each one," "everybody," "everyone," "many a man," which, though implying more than one person, requires the pronoun to be in the singular. Similar to this, but with even less justification, is the use of the plural pronoun with the antecedent "anybody," "anyone," "somebody," "someone," the intention being either to avoid the awkward "he or she" or to avoid committing oneself to either. Some bashful speakers even say, "A friend of mine told me that they, etc." Use "he" with all the above words, unless the antecedent is or must be feminine. [I have kept this for historical interest as much as for any other reason. For the official view represented in this book, please see what I say on the subject in the Preface.]

Very. Use this word sparingly. Where emphasis is necessary, use words strong in themselves.

Viewpoint. Write "point of view," but do not misuse this, as many do, for "view" or "opinion."

While. Avoid the indiscriminate use of this word for "and," "but," and "although." Many writers use it frequently as a substitute for "and" or "but," either from a mere desire to vary the connective or from uncertainty about which of the two connectives is the more appropriate. In this use it is best replaced by a semicolon. Thus,

> "The office and salesrooms are on the ground
> floor, while the rest of the building is devoted
> to manufacturing" should be "The office and
> salesrooms are on the ground floor; the rest of the
> building is devoted to manufacturing."

Its use as a virtual equivalent of "although" is allowable in sentences where this leads to no ambiguity or absurdity. Therefore "While I admire his energy, I wish it were employed in a better cause," is entirely correct, as shown by the paraphrase, "I admire his energy; at the same time I wish it were employed in a better cause."

Compare: "While the temperature reaches 90 or 95 degrees in the daytime, the nights are often chilly," with "Although the temperature reaches 90 or 95 degrees in the daytime, the nights are often chilly." The paraphrase "The temperature reaches 90 or 95 degrees in the daytime; at the same time the nights are often chilly" shows why the use of "while" is incorrect.

In general, the writer will do well to use "while" only with strict literalness, in the sense of "during the time that."

Whom. Often incorrectly used for "who" before "he said" or similar expressions, when it is really the *subject* of a later verb in the clause. Thus:

"His brother, whom he said would send him the
money" should be "His brother, who he said would
send him the money."

"The man whom he thought was his friend" should be
"The man who (that) he thought was his friend" or
". . . whom he thought his friend."

Worth while *or* **worthwhile.** Overworked as a term
of vague approval and (with "not") of disapproval. It is
strictly applicable only to actions, as in "Is it worth while
(or worthwhile) to telegraph?" Therefore "His books are
not worthwhile" should be "His books are not worth reading" or "not worth one's while to read" or ". . . do not repay
reading."

The use of "worthwhile" before a noun ("a worthwhile
story") is indefensible.

Would. A conditional statement in the *first* person requires "should," not "would," as in "I should not have succeeded without his help." Also, the equivalent of "shall" in
indirect quotation after a verb in the past tense is "should,"
not "would," as in "He predicted that before long we should
have a great surprise." To express habitual or repeated action, the past tense, without "would," is usually sufficient,
and from its brevity, more emphatic. Therefore "Once a
year he would visit the old mansion" is better as "Once a
year he visited the old mansion."

PART III

Appendices:
Some Useful Lists

Inventory of Definitions of Grammatical Terms

Most of the definitions that have been an important part of this book are collected here for two practical reasons. One is to make it easier to find quickly any particular definition being sought. The other is to make it easier to set about learning by heart those definitions that need to be learnt by heart.

In the latter context, I should like to stress even more strongly what I have said earlier in this book about learning definitions. Whether you are six years old or sixty or more, those definitions given in bold print need to be learnt *exactly,* including even the word order and the inclusion or exclusion of words such as "the."

This is because, unless the definitions are learnt as exactly as this, they tend not to be impressed firmly enough in the mind to remain there. They can be forgotten at least to the extent of important details in them being lost. And leaving out any important detail of a definition makes the definition largely useless.

When to start learning the grammar definitions by heart? The earlier the better, and that, contrary to modern supposition, includes before the child is capable of understanding what is being learnt. It is indeed all the better for it to be done then. The period before the so-called age of reason, which on average is reached at around seven years old, is the period in a human life during which learning is done much more easily than later on, and when, after all, the child's mind is only *starting* to become capable of the educating that needs the full use of the intellect. It is also the best time to train the memory.

Furthermore, and to reiterate what I said in Chapter 3 of Part I, contrary to what is often supposed, children typically relish doing it. If you doubt me, you might like to visit the Gwynne Teaching Web site. There you will see some of my youngest pupils reciting—sometimes for considerable periods of time—things they do not yet understand, such as multiplication tables and Latin nouns and verbs, often smiling enthusiastically as they do so.

> Accidence/morphology deals with how words are formed and especially with how words *change their form*—most often their endings—when they are used for different purposes.

Adjectives. An *adjective* is a word which describes a noun or a pronoun.

Adjectives, comparative. A *comparative adjective* is the form of the positive adjective which makes it mean *more* of the adjective in question.

Adjectives, positive. A *positive adjective* is a word which describes a noun or a pronoun.

Adjectives, superlative. A *superlative adjective* is the form of the positive adjective which makes it mean *the most* of the adjective in question. In conversational English it can sometimes mean "very," as in "That information is most useful."

Adverbs. An *adverb* is a word which modifies a verb, an adjective or another adverb. The main kinds of adverbs are adverbs of *time* (when), adverbs of *place* (where), adverbs of *manner* (how), and adverbs of *degree* (for instance, "very," "too" and "so"), though there are also adverbs which do not fit into any category, such as "however" (as in "*However* difficult grammar may seem at first"), "either" (as in "Don't you like learning grammar *either*?"), "just" (as in "Grammar is *just* so much fun") and also adverbs which modify whole clauses, such as "admittedly" and "actually." Most adverbs can have comparatives and superlatives ("more beautifully" and "most beautifully"). Adverbs are very often formed by adding "-ly" on to the end of adjectives (as in "quickly" but not as in "fast").

Auxiliary verbs. See **Verbs, auxiliary** and **Verbs, modal.**

Clauses. A *clause* is a group of words with a verb in it. A *clause* can be a *noun-clause,* an *adjective-clause* or an *adverb-clause.*

Complements. A *complement* is the noun, pronoun or adjective which completes the sentence or clause after a *being* word.

Conjunctions. A *conjunction* is a word which joins together any two words of the same part of speech, or any two phrases, or clauses, or even sentences. There are two kinds of conjunctions: coordinating conjunctions and subordinating conjunctions.

Conjunctions, co-ordinating. *Co-ordinating conjunctions* are conjunctions which connect to each other *clauses of the same rank,* whether *main clauses* or *subsidiary clauses.* There are very few of them: "and," "but," "or," "nor" and even sometimes—especially in American English—"yet."

Conjunctions, subordinating. *Subordinating conjunctions* are conjunctions which connect subsidiary clauses to main clauses and subsidiary clauses to higher-ranking subsidiary clauses (that is, subsidiary clauses which they modify). Examples: "after," "before," "because," "as," "for" (when it means "because"), "since" (in both its meanings as a conjunction), "although," "in order that," "unless,"

"until," "while," "when," "whenever," "where,"
"wherever," "why" and the relative pronouns "who"
and "which."

Co-ordinating conjunctions. See Conjunctions,
co-ordinating.

Definition. A *definition* is a statement of the precise
nature of something or the precise meaning of
a word or phrase. Specifically in grammar, a
definition is a statement of the exact meaning of
a word or phrase that sufficiently distinguishes it
from any other word or phrase, preferably in the
fewest possible words.

Gerundives. See Verbs, non-finite parts of. The
gerundive.

Gerunds. See Verbs, non-finite parts of. The gerund.

Imperatives. See Verbs, moods. The *imperative
mood.*

Infinitives. See Verbs, moods. The *infinitive,* and
Verbs, non-finite parts of. The infinitive.

Interrogative mood. See Verbs, moods. The
interrogative mood.

Modal verbs. See Verbs, modal, and also Verbs,
auxiliary.

Mood, imperative. See Verbs, moods. The *imperative
mood.*

Mood, indicative. See Verbs, moods. The *indicative
mood.*

Mood, infinitive. See Verbs, moods. The *infinitive.*

Mood, interrogative. See Verbs, moods. The
interrogative mood.

Mood, subjunctive. See Verbs, moods. The
subjunctive mood.

Morphology deals with how words are formed and
especially with how words *change* their form—
most often their endings—when they are used for
different purposes. P. ?·3

Nouns. A *noun* is the name of a person, place or thing.

Nouns, abstract. An *abstract noun* is the name of
something that we cannot perceive with our senses,
because it is separate from matter.

Nouns, collective. A *collective noun* denotes a group
of persons or things of a particular kind.

Nouns, concrete. A *concrete noun* is the name of
something which exists in a *material* form and which
we can therefore see, hear, touch, taste or smell.

Objects, direct. The *direct object* is that which
undergoes what the subject of the sentence or the
clause does; *or* the person or thing to which an
action or feeling is directed; *or* the part of a sentence
or clause which follows the main verb if that verb
is a transitive verb and which corresponds to the
subject of a passive clause or sentence.

Objects, indirect. An *indirect object* is a noun or
pronoun only *indirectly* affected by the verb it
follows, as in "He teaches grammar *to me*" and "He
bought some grammar books *for me,*" which can

also be worded as "He teaches me grammar" and "He bought me some grammar books."

Participles. See Verbs, non-finite parts of. The participle.

Phrases. A *phrase* is a group of words *without* a verb in it. A phrase can be a *noun-phrase,* an *adjective-phrase,* an *adverb-phrase,* a *preposition-phrase,* even an *interjection-phrase* (as in "Heavens above!").

Predicates. The *predicate* of a sentence or clause is whatever is said about the subject.

Pronouns. A *pronoun* is a word which stands in place of a noun.

Pronouns, conjunctive. Examples: "He *who* dares" and "The thing *that* he dares to do," and, joining two clauses together, "We have found the house *that* you were looking for." Also known as relative pronouns.

Pronouns, demonstrative. Examples: "this" and "that," as in "To be or not to be: *that* is the question."

Pronouns, indefinite. Examples: "I can see neither *anyone* nor *anything* of any importance" and "I can see *someone* and *something* of some importance."

Pronouns, intensive. Example: "I *myself* can see it."

Pronouns, interrogative. Examples: "who," "whoever," "which" and "what," as in "*Who* dares?" "Whoever can it have been who made that noise?" "*Which* of you made that noise?" and "What is the time?"

Pronouns, possessive. Examples: "mine," "yours," "thine," "his," "hers," "its," "ours," "yours" (this time plural), "theirs," as in "Yes, this book of *yours* really is *yours.*"

Pronouns–possessive adjectives, usually so called. Examples: "my," "your," "thy," "his," "her," "its," "our," "your" and "their," when standing (a) before the noun(s) they apply to (as in "*your* grammar lessons"); or (b) before any adjectives that go immediately before the noun(s) they apply to (as in "*your* valuable grammar lessons"); or (c) before adverbs in the cases where an adverb is before an adjective which is before a noun (as in "*your* wonderfully valuable grammar lessons").

Pronouns, reflexive. Example: "I myself can see *myself.*"

Pronouns, relative. Examples: "He *who* dares," "The thing *that* he dares to do," and, joining two clauses together, "We have found the house *that* you were looking for." Also known as conjunctive pronouns.

Sentences. A *sentence* is a word or group of words expressing a complete statement, wish, command or question, whether as a thought, or in speech, or in writing; *or* a group of words ending in a period, an exclamation mark or a question mark.

Subjects. The *subject* of a sentence or clause is who or what the sentence or clause is all about.

Subordinating conjunctions. See **Conjunctions, subordinating.**

Syntax deals with the *use* made of words, especially when words are used in combination.

Tenses. See **Verbs, tenses.**

Verbs. A *verb* is a doing or being word, *or* a *verb* is a word that expresses an action or a state.

Verbs, auxiliary. **Auxiliary verbs** are verbs used with other verbs to form some of the parts of the other verbs. Examples: "*am* learning," "*do* learn," "*will be* learning," "*have* learnt." Some grammarians also include under this heading what are sometimes known as **modal verbs.** See **Verbs, modal.**

Verbs, intransitive. An *intransitive verb* is a doing verb that does not take a direct object, as in the sentence "I come and I go." With such verbs, the doer's action *stops with the doer,* involving no one and nothing else.

Verbs, modal. **Modal verbs** are verbs used for modal concepts such as what is *possible* (for instance, "can" and "could," "may" and "might"); what is *necessary* ("must"); what is *allowed* ("may" and "might" again); and what is *expected* or *intended* ("may" and "might" again and also "will" and "shall").

Verbs, moods. A *mood* is the manner, or "mode," in which a verb is used to express a statement, a question, a command or a doubt. **The *indicative***

mood is used for *making a statement* or *asking a question* (as in "I learn" and "Am I learning?"). Some grammarians would give a different mood for questions, the *interrogative mood*. The *imperative mood* is (a) for *commands* (as in *"Stop!"*) and (b) for when one *begs* or *entreats* (as in "*Help* me, please, if you can"). The *subjunctive mood,* sometimes in English and always in Latin and Greek and some other languages, is used when expressing *doubt, improbability, uncertainty,* an *order,* a *wish* or *recommendation,* a *condition* or a *purpose.* Examples: (1) "If it *were* known that grammar was so important, more people *would* study it." (2) "I *should do* it if I *were* you." (3) "I have recommended to him that he *make* more effort." (4) "Resolved that the learning of grammar *be* everywhere promoted." (5) The idiomatic "If need *be,*" "*Suffice* it to say," and "*Come* what may." The *infinitive* is often included under the heading of moods. It is used to express an action or state of being without giving any indication of a subject for the action or state (as in "to learn" and "to have been taught"). See also in the next paragraph for a fuller explanation.

Verbs, non-finite parts of. The infinitive names the action or state without reference to who or what *is* either (a) *doing* the action or (b) *being* whatever it is that he, she or it is being. Examples: "to teach" (present indefinite active); "to be about to be teaching" (future indicative active and future continuous active); "to have been taught" (perfect indicative passive). The participle is a part of a verb that does the job of an adjective as well as the job of a verb (as in "the *teaching* profession," "children *being taught*"). The gerund is a verbal noun, as in "*Seeing* is *believing*," "They like learning," and "You are good at learning." The gerundive is a verbal adjective—meaning "ought to be," "suitable for"—that is only seen in English when the original, untranslated Latin is used, as in *agenda, memorandum* and *Miranda.*

Verbs, tenses. A *tense* is the form of a verb which shows *when* the action *is being* done, *might* be done, *should* be done, etc., or *when* the state *is in being, may be in being,* etc.

Verbs, transitive. A *transitive verb* is a doing verb that needs a *direct object.*

Verbs, voices. *Doing* verbs are in either the active voice or the passive voice. The *active voice* of a *transitive verb* is for when the subject of a sentence or clause is *doing* whatever is being done (as in "I learn"). The *passive voice* is for when the subject is not *doing* the action but *experiencing* it—that is, having it done to him, her, it or them (as in "We are being taught").

Voice, active. See Verbs, voices.

Voice, passive. See Verbs, voices.

CHAPTER 2

The Irregular Verbs

The following aims at being a complete list. It may be noted that except where the verbs have prefixes as in "awake," "misspell" and "understand," they are all single-syllable words and almost always single-syllable in the past tense and past participle as well as in the base form.

Because some irregular verbs are less common than others, the most common ones are highlighted as the ones to be learnt first so that improvement in some of the commonest usages in the English language can be as quick as possible. Where two alternatives are given, the first one is the normal usage in Britain. In America, the second one tends to be more normal.

Learning these by heart is much to be preferred to picking them up gradually, which in any case is not always done accurately.

Base Form	Past Tense	Past Participle
awake	awoke	awoken
be	was, were	been
bear	bore	borne
beat	beat	beaten/beat*
become	became	become
begin	began	begun
bend	bent	bent
beset	beset	beset
bet	bet	bet
bid	bid/bade	bid/bidden
bind	bound	bound
bite	bit	bitten
bleed	bled	bled
blow	blew	blown
break	broke	broken
breed	bred	bred
bring	brought	brought
broadcast	broadcast	broadcast
build	built	built
burn	burnt/burned	burnt/burned
burst	burst	burst
buy	bought	bought
cast	cast	cast
catch	caught	caught
choose	chose	chosen

* Except in "dead beat" when used as the past participle rather than as a noun or an adjective.

cling	clung	clung
come	came	come
cost	cost	cost
creep	crept	crept
cut	cut	cut
deal	dealt	dealt
dig	dug	dug
dive	dived	dived
do	did	done
draw	drew	drawn
dream	dreamt/dreamed	dreamt/dreamed
drink	drank	drunk
drive	drove	driven
eat	ate	eaten
fall	fell	fallen
feed	fed	fed
feel	felt	felt
fight	fought	fought
find	found	found
fit	fit	fit
flee	fled	fled
fling	flung	flung
fly	flew	flown
forbid	forbade	forbidden
forget	forgot	forgotten
forgive	forgave	forgiven
forgo	forwent	forgone
forsake	forsook	forsaken

freeze	froze	frozen
get	got	got/gotten*
give	gave	given
go	went	gone
grind	ground	ground
grow	grew	grown
hang	hung	hung ←
have	had	had
hear	heard	heard
hide	hid	hidden
hit	hit	hit
hold	held	held
hurt	hurt	hurt
keep	kept	kept
kneel	knelt/kneeled	knelt/kneeled
knit	knitted/knit	knitted/knit
know	knew	known
lay	laid	laid
lead	led	led
leap	leapt/leaped	leapt/leaped
learn	learnt/learned	learnt/learned
leave	left	left
lend	lent	lent
let	let	let
lie	lay	lain
light	lit/lighted	lit/lighted

* "Gotten" is archaic in England though not in the United States.

lose	lost	lost
make	made	made
mean	meant	meant
meet	met	met
misspell	misspelt/misspelled	misspelt/misspelled
mistake	mistook	mistaken
mow	mowed	mown/mowed
overcome	overcame	overcome
overdo	overdid	overdone
overtake	overtook	overtaken
overthrow	overthrew	overthrown
pay	paid	paid
prove	proved	proved/proven
put	put	put
quit	quit	quit
read	read	read
rid	rid	rid/ridden
ride	rode	ridden
ring	rang	rung
rise	rose	risen
run	ran	run
saw	sawed	sawn/sawed
say	said	said
see	saw	seen
seek	sought	sought
sell	sold	sold
send	sent	sent
set	set	set

sew	sewed	sewn
shake	shook	shaken
shave	shaved	shaved/shaven
shear	sheared/shore*	shorn
shed	shed	shed
shine	shone	shone
shoe	shod/shoed	shod/shoed
shoot	shot	shot
show	showed	shown/showed
shrink	shrank	shrunk
shut	shut	shut
sing	sang	sung
sink	sank	sunk
sit	sat	sat
slay	slew	slain
sleep	slept	slept
slide	slid	slid
sling	slung	slung
slit	slit	slit
smite	smote	smitten
sow	sowed	sown/sowed
speak	spoke	spoken
speed	sped	sped
spend	spent	spent
spill	spilt/spilled	spilt/spilled
spin	spun	spun

* Archaic.

spit	spat/spit	spat/spit
split	split	split
spread	spread	spread
spring	sprang	sprung
stand	stood	stood
steal	stole	stolen
stick	stuck	stuck
sting	stung	stung
stink	stank	stunk
stride	strode	stridden
strike	struck	struck
string	strung	strung
strive	strove	striven
swear	swore	sworn
sweep	swept	swept
swell	swelled	swollen/swelled
swim	swam	swum
swing	swung	swung
take	took	taken
teach	taught	taught
tear	tore	torn
tell	told	told
think	thought	thought
thrive	thrived	thrived
throw	threw	thrown
thrust	thrust	thrust
tread	trod	trodden
understand	understood	understood

uphold	upheld	upheld
upset	upset	upset
wake	woke	woken
wear	wore	worn
weave	wove/weaved	woven/weaved
wed	wedded/wed	wedded/wed
weep	wept	wept
win	won	won
wind	wound	wound
withhold	withheld	withheld
withstand	withstood	withstood
wring	wrung	wrung
write	wrote	written

CHAPTER 3

Special Prepositions Needed by Particular Words

There are certain verbs, nouns and adjectives which require special prepositions. Sometimes they are important simply because to use the wrong preposition is illiterate, as "different to something" is wrong, as is "different than something" (though "different than" when followed by a clause is strongly argued by many—see below), and "different from something" is correct. Sometimes use of a different preposition will change the meaning of the word that the preposition follows.

Abhorrence for
Absolve from
Accord with
Acquit of

Adapted for (by nature)

Adapted to (intentionally)

Affinity between

Agree to (a proposal)

Agree with (a person)

Bestow upon

Change for (a thing)

Change with (a person)

Comply with

Confer on (means "give to")

Confer with (means "talk with")

Confide in (means "trust in")

Confide to (means "entrust to")

Conform to

In conformity with

Convenient for (a purpose)

Convenient to (a person)

Conversant with

Correspond to (a thing)

Correspond with (a person)

Dependent on (but independent of)

Derogatory to

Differ from (a statement or opinion)

Differ with (a person)

Different from (see the discussion on what may follow
    "different" at the foot of this list.)

Disappointed by, in or with (someone or something)

Disappointed of (what we cannot get)

Dissent from
Exception from (a rule)
Exception to (a statement)
Glad at (a piece of news)
Glad of (a possession)
Involve in
Martyr for (a cause)
Martyr to (a disease)
Need of or for
Part from (a person)
Part with (a thing)
Profit by
Reconcile to (a person)
Reconcile with (a statement)
A taste for (art)
Taste of (food)
Thirst for or after (knowledge)

Of those listed above, "different" is a special case. Acknowledged authorities on grammar are by no means in agreement about what prepositions can and cannot follow it, rival candidates being "from," "to" and "than." After reviewing the evidence, this author dares to pronounce as follows.

"Different from" is always right and safe. "Different to," much used in England but scarcely in America, is always wrong. The fact that no one would ever say that something "differs to something else" rather than "differs from something else" is useful, if not infallible, evidence against "different to."

"Different than," as common in America as "different to" is in England, has enjoyed a long history of occasional use even by highly regarded writers. Some American grammarians, including ones who acknowledge that it is technically unorthodox, offer a special defence for it when it is followed by clauses. Some even go so far as to say (a) use "from" after a noun or pronoun, as in "this book is different *from mine*"; (b) use "than" before a clause with a subject and a verb, as in "this book is different *than I expected.*" Those who favour "than" before a clause have, moreover, a superficially useful argument: it avoids the slight awkwardness of "different from what I expected" and the greater awkwardness of "different from that which . . ." In other words, before a noun or pronoun, "than" is being used as a preposition, while before a clause it is being used as a conjunction.

Readers of this book who have the commendable prescriptive instincts that I have been trying to encourage will fight it in both instances, however.

In the first place, "than" is not truly a preposition but *only* a conjunction. A "quasi-preposition" is the term that the traditional *Concise Oxford Dictionary* gives to its secondary use as preposition, reflecting the fact that the usage "She is older than him" is very much more common than the strictly correct "She is older than he (is)," with the second "is" either expressed or understood. This means that "different than mine," with "than" playing the role of a preposition, cannot be right.

In the second place, "than" even as a conjunction is only used when introducing the second item of two things being compared; in other words, almost invariably after a comparative adjective or adverb. Logically, therefore, although you can say "This book is *better* than I expected," you cannot say "This book is *different* than I expected." You would need the word "more" in front of "different"—which would of course convey a different meaning—to make it grammatical.

What about the relative awkwardness of "This book is *different* from what I expected," which can be even more awkward in more complicated constructions, as when the eighteenth-century author Samuel Richardson wrote "a very different Pamela than I used to leave all company and pleasure for"?

The straightforward answer is that not much rewording of the sentence will be needed to avoid the awkwardness, but even if this involves taking some trouble, so be it. Never do I suggest that hard, painstaking work is not involved in the efforts needed to practice as effectively as possible the all-important skill of communicating. Rather, the encouragement that I offer is that whatever work is involved is overwhelmingly worth it and also that this work gradually becomes progressively easier as the skills involved become more habitual and indeed as making the necessary effort becomes more habitual. "Careful polishing of what we have written," I included as one of the elements of producing good style, in my Foreword to the section by Strunk. I repeat that here. On this specific point, you could consider, for instance, "a very different Pamela from the Pamela for whom I used to leave all company and pleasure" and, if not satisfied with that, set about improving it further.

CHAPTER 4

The Formation of Plurals

1. There are three chief ways of forming the plural in English:

a. By adding *es* or *s* to the singular. Examples: "box," "boxes"; "gas," "gases"; "loaf," "loaves"; "witch," "witches"; "shelf," "shelves"; "hero," "heroes"; "lady," "ladies"; "thief," "thieves."

Note the following:

i. Nouns ending in *f* commonly change the *f* into *v*, but we say "roofs," "cliffs," "dwarfs," "chiefs" and so on.

ii. The letter *y* with a vowel before it is not changed in the plural. Examples: "keys," "valleys," "chimneys," "days."

iii. The letter *y* with a consonant before it *is* changed

in the plural. Examples: "ladies," "rubies," "soliloquies."

b. By adding *en.* Examples: "oxen," "children," "brethren."

c. By changing the vowel sound. Examples: "man," "men"; "foot," "feet"; "goose," "geese"; "tooth," "teeth"; "mouse," "mice"; "louse," "lice."

2. Some nouns are the same in the plural as in the singular. Examples: "deer," "sheep," "cod," "trout," "mackerel."

3. A few words are false plurals: singulars which look like plurals. Examples: "alms" (meaning a donation) and "riches" (meaning "wealth").

4. A few plurals are treated as singulars. Examples: "amends" (as in "make *much*—not many—amends"); "gallows" (as in "more than *one* gallows"); "news" (as in "*much* news"); "odds" (as in "it doesn't make *much* odds"); "pains" (as in "take *much* pains"); "shambles" (as in the cliché "*one* almighty shambles").

5. Many nouns can be used only in the plural. They fall into two categories:

a. Names of things consisting of two or more parts. These are "bellows," "drawers," "jeans," "lungs," "pincers," "pliers," "scissors," "shears," "snuffers," "spectacles" and "glasses" (meaning "spectacles"), "tongs," "trousers" and "tweezers." Some of these, such as "drawer," "glass" and "spectacle," change their meaning entirely in the singular.

b. Names of things that are taken in the mass. These are "annals," "archives," "ashes," "assets," "dregs," "embers," "entrails," "hustings," "lees" (meaning the sediment of wine), "measles," "molasses," "mumps," "oats," "staggers" and "victuals."

6. Many nouns have been brought into the English language from other languages, some of them naturalised and having adopted English plurals, some of them keeping their original plurals.

a. Examples of imports that now have, or at least can have, English plurals: bandits (originally "banditti"), "cherubs" and "seraphs" ("cherubim" and "seraphim"), "dogmas" ("dogmata"), "focuses" ("foci"), "formulas" ("formulae"), "indexes" ("indices") in one of the senses of the word "index" (see below), "memorandums" ("memoranda") and "terminuses" ("terminae").

b. Examples of imports keep, or at least can keep, their own plurals, not always perfectly:

i. Latin words: "datum," "data"; "formula," "formulae"; "genus," "genera"; "series," "series"; "species," "species"; and "stratum," "strata."

ii. Greek words: "analysis," "analyses"; "axis,"
   "axes"; "ellipsis," "ellipses"; "parenthesis,"
   "parentheses"; and "phenomenon," "phenomena."
iii. French words: "monsieur," "messieurs"; and
   "madame," "mesdames."
iv. Italian words: "bandit," "banditti"; "dilettante,"
   "dilettanti"; "libretto," "libretti"; and "virtuoso,"
   "virtuosi."
v. Hebrew words: "cherub," "cherubim"; and
   "seraph," "seraphim."

7. Compound words sometimes put the first word into the plural and not the second, sometimes the second word and not the first, and sometimes both. There are two rules to show which category a compound word belongs to, and one category where one simply has to learn its very few instances:

a. When one of the words is clearly the leading
   word. Examples: "sons-in-law," "hangers-on" and
   "lookers-on."
   (In the United States, "attorney general" and
   "major general" are most often treated as two words
   and not hyphenated, and the plural of "court-
   martial" is usually "courts-martial.")
b. It is difficult to identify a rule under which
   occasionally both parts of the compound are in the
   plural, as with "menservants" and "lords-justices."

8. Finally, several nouns have two plurals, each giving a radically different meaning. Examples: "brother": "brothers" (by blood) and "brethren" (of a community); "cloth": "cloths" (kinds of cloth) and "clothes" (garments); "die": "dies" (stamps for coining) and "dice" (cubes for gaming); "fish": "fishes" (looked at separately) and "fish" (taken collectively); "genius": "geniuses" (men of talent) and "genii" (powerful spirits); "index": "indexes" (to books) and "indices" (to quantities in algebra); "penny": "pennies" (taken separately) and "pence" (taken collectively); "shot": "shots" (separate discharges) and "shot" (pellets, collectively).

Further Reading

Very much more comprehensive works on English grammar than would be suitable for the particular job this book sets out to do are the two classics by J. C. Nesfield. Covering everything on the subject of writing English, including even the composition of poetry, his *Manual of English Grammar and Composition* was originally published by Macmillan in 1898, then revised by Frederick T. Wood in 1963 and republished by Macmillan in 1964, and reprinted many times since. It is no longer in print but is not difficult to find secondhand. At the relatively elementary level, his *Outline of English Grammar,* originally published by Macmillan in 1908, and republished by Elibron Classics Replica in 2007, is still in print. Not surprisingly given that both are more than a hundred years old, they can be recommended as free from even the most insignificant errors, which is by no means the case with all the books recommended, however enthusiastically, below.

The best American equivalent of Nesfield's *Outline of English Grammar* is probably John C. Hodges's *Harbrace*

Handbook of English (Harcourt, Brace, 1941)—but only in editions up to but *excluding* the revised thirteenth edition; subsequent editions have been spoilt by "modernisation."

To the best of my knowledge, there has never been anything published in America that is as comprehensive and useful as Nesfield's *Manual of English Grammar and Composition,* and indeed I know of an academic institution in America in which Nesfield's *Manual* is used as its English grammar textbook. The nearest equivalent is the generally excellent *Writing and Thinking* by Norman Foerster and J. M. Steadman Jr. (Expanded Edition, Paper Tiger, 2000; the original, Houghton Mifflin, 1941).

Other books that I have found exceptionally valuable, some of them referred to in the preceding pages:

The Third Edition of Strunk's *The Elements of Style— with Revisions, an Introduction, and a Chapter on Writing* by E. B. White, first published in 1979 and still in print. The problems for British readers caused by its having been written for American readers are few and tiny compared with its usefulness.

Style Guide, "based on the house style of the *Economist* newspaper" (Profile, most recent edition, the tenth, 2010), is a marvel both in the range of topics it covers and in the soundness—often even defying today's standard political correctness—with which it treats them. Amongst much else, it includes a section highlighting the important differences between British and American syntax, punctuation, spelling and usage. It is kept constantly updated with new editions. One never knows when a new edition is going to appear which has been revised to conform with present-day fashion at the expense of literacy, but I can confirm that *Style Guide* has been free from such defects at least up to its tenth edition.

A Dictionary of Modern English Usage by H. W. Fowler has been, justifiably, so influential that it has for long been sufficiently identified simply by the title "Fowler." It is endlessly useful and also thoroughly entertaining, and I recommend it, even though it is not invariably completely reliable in its judgements, as in the deplorable passage that it pained me to draw attention to in Chapter 6 of Part I.

My enthusiastic recommendation applies only to the first two editions of it, however, and very much not to the 2004 edition edited by R. W. Burchfield, eminent though Burchfield is, having been Chief Editor of the Oxford English dictionaries and an editor of *The Cambridge History of the English Language.* Indeed, other than to help sales, it is not easy to see what justification there is for "Fowler" being part of the title, since Burchfield's edition includes little of what Fowler wrote—"Fowler's name remains on the title-page, even though his book has been largely rewritten," Burchfield himself says in the Preface. The new "Fowler" has been rewritten, moreover, largely *in opposition* to Fowler. Burchfield is actually dismissive of the original: although "a masterpiece," it has long been "a fossil," he claims, before, for instance, proceeding to refer to grossly substandard English, such as "gotta," "kinda" and "didn't ought," as becoming "more common," without a hint of disapproval or indication that they *are* substandard English. As I say, it is only the "Fowler" that really *is* "Fowler" that I recommend.

Plain Words, published in 1948, and *ABC of Plain Words,* published in 1951, are two small books that were written by Sir Ernest Gowers, a distinguished civil servant as well as scholar, at the invitation of the British Treasury for the purpose of helping to improve official English. Although they cover a more limited field than the others mentioned so far, I unreservedly recommend them. They are not only as authoritative and tried and tested as any grammar textbooks could be but also stimulating and thoroughly enjoyable for their elegance and wit.

Avoid, though, the editions of *The Complete Plain Words,* combining the two in one volume, that are most easily available today. The first edition is fine—authentic Gowers. In the second edition, revised by Sir Bruce Fraser, already some of the best features of Gowers were lost. In the third edition, further revised by Sidney Greenbaum and Janet Whitcut, much more still has been lost. The originals (or the first combined edition) may be difficult to find, but they are worth searching for.

Disappointingly, considering how beneficial his influence has been overall, even uncontaminated Gowers is not always reliable. For instance, he mounts an emphatic case for the legitimacy of the split infinitive. At least he argues his side as well as he can, rather than simply dismissing the objection to it as pedantic. I urge readers who favour his position to compare his reasoning and evidence with those of my ultimate hero among modern writers on the subject of English grammar, Professor Dummett, in the volume by him that I shall be coming to shortly, and to see for themselves, if only from that one example, whether my unconditional admiration for Dummett is justified.

Strictly English by Simon Heffer (Random House, 2010) is another book that can justly be described as a marvel, not least because its author is *not* a Burchfield-type liberal in language matters. Completely up to date with modern developments in English, it not only spells out what constitutes good English but also *confronts* just about every example of bad English in common and widely accepted use today and in some places does so even more persuasively than the wonderful *Style Guide*. (I say "*just about* every example" because I can find no reference in the book to the grossly illiterate but almost universal "per capita" in place of the correct "per caput.") *Strictly English* is very widely researched, covers a huge amount of ground (some of it different from the ground covered in *Style Guide*), is competently argued when it needs to be, and is always very readable. Not the least of its merits is a bibliography at the end, which not only is reasonably comprehensive but also includes useful descriptions of each book referred to.

As already just indicated, in many ways my favourite of all of the modern writers on the English language is

Professor Michael Dummett in his *Grammar and Style: For Examination Candidates and Others* (Duckworth, 1993). Although still in print more than twenty years after it was first published, and therefore presumably at least a steady seller, the book is remarkably little known—for instance, it does not feature in Simon Heffer's otherwise very comprehensive bibliography.

Professor Dummett was neither a professional teacher of English nor even, with only one other book to his name, a remotely prolific writer. A professor of logic at Oxford (Wykeham Professor of Logic Emeritus), he was, in a sense, provoked into writing *Grammar and Style* by what he had experienced as a Finals examiner at Oxford and then had been observing in casual newspaper reading, "particularly of the Quality press." Tackling every single contentious point that his wide range of current reading had brought to his attention, he used his training in logic to good effect. Never does he look at a disputed item without examining it carefully enough to get to the bottom of it, and if necessary contradicting what is said by authoritative authors of the past. Never, either, does he disappoint by getting something wrong, which, with so much detail involved, is all too difficult to avoid in a first edition. Always one can recognise from the logic with which he backs up his conclusions that what he is saying is completely sound. The manner in which he argues towards his conclusions is enjoyably penetrating as well.

In many ways, the most deeply satisfying textbooks

on all aspects of English are older ones, dating back into the nineteenth century, which do not normally feature in bibliographies of modern grammars. There is even something comforting about them—one *knows,* as one opens them, that the authors are completely on top of the subject and that there are going to be no mistakes or serious misjudgements.

The English Language: Its Grammar, History, and Literature, by J. M. D. Meiklejohn, Professor of the Theory, History and Practice of Education in the University of St. Andrews (Alfred M. Holden, 1894), to which I referred in the Preface, is my favourite for its extraordinary comprehensiveness and thoroughness. Other very useful books of the nineteenth and early twentieth century are:

The Grammar, History, and Derivation of the English Language, with Chapters on Parsing, Analysis of Sentences and Prosody, by the Rev. Canon Evan Daniel, M.A., Principal of the National Society's Training College, Battersea (National Society's Depository, 1890).

A School Manual of English Grammar with Copious Exercises, by William Smith and Theophilus Hall (John Murray, 10th edition, 1889).

The Elements of English Grammar, with a Chapter on Essay-Writing, by Alfred S. West (Cambridge University Press, 1910).

A Matriculation English Course, by Lancelot Oliphant (Gregg, 1928, and revised and expanded edition, 1935, and again in 1948).

School Certificate English, by A. E. M. Bayliss (rev. ed., George G. Harrap, revised edition, 1943).

Finally, perhaps the most interesting book of all dealing with English grammar is *The Philosophy of Grammar* by Otto Jespersen, first published in 1924. It is not necessary reading for the purpose of improving the ability to compose English. Its target is the subject of grammar in itself, and it makes a magnificent and enthralling job of putting every aspect of grammatical theory under a microscope and, again and again, exposing weaknesses in even the most straightforward rules that one would never have suspected. It is a book more suitable for those who have gained a good mastery of the science of writing rather than for those who are still on the journey there.

Acknowledgements

My debt to Mr. Tom Hodgkinson I have already made clear in the Preface. But for him the book would have been neither thought of, nor given its present title, nor published in the first three editions that have led to this one.

Very much instrumental in refining this book as it was being compiled have been my wife, Frederica, and my daughter and teaching partner, Chloe. I shall allow myself to slip into the intellectual gutter of present-day vernacular, for only the second time in this book, to say gratefully that their constant help, when they had much else on their plates, has been brilliant, amazing, awesome and "wicked." Thank you, ladies.

Ebury's representative responsible for all aspects of getting this book into your hands, Mr. Jake Lingwood, has been helpful as well as unfailingly efficient to a degree that I have actually found startling, especially after stories I have heard of other authors' experiences with their publishers. He was consistently frank but gentle in his always sound criticisms, and painstaking, encouraging, enthusiastic and considerate. Lucky you, if you are ever an author of a book worth publishing and Providence sends you Mr. Lingwood's way.

Lucky you, too, if Mr. Lingwood should arrange for your book to be copyedited by Mrs. Mary Chamberlain. No error or area of doubt was too small or too subtle to escape her notice, and her suggestions were invariably helpful and often constructive and valuable. Anyone who thinks it even remotely possible that I am being as enthusiastic as this simply to be consistent with my tone in the other acknowledgements here is welcome to take advantage of modern technology and ask me to e-mail a few pages of my original draft to Mrs. Chamberlain and then to compare them with the equivalent pages in this book, to see what a difference she made.

Happy also has consistently been my first experience with an agent. From the moment I was introduced to Miss Cat Ledger, and more and more as time has gone on, I have felt fortunate to have at my side the advantage of her experience, attention to detail, patience and, when needed, persistence. She was also never too busy to be available at short notice as my pleasurable relationship with Ebury was developing.

Finally, there is the matter of my experience with Alfred A. Knopf, Inc., the publisher in the United States of this expanded edition. Perhaps the best way of making clear my appreciation is to say that, throughout, my relationship with all those there with whom this book has brought me into contact has been in every way as satisfactory, agreeable and "special" as my relationship with those of Ebury Press. At, doubtless, the cost of those at Knopf blushing modestly as they read these words, I shall name them: Mr. George Andreou, editor; Miss Victoria Pearson, production editor; Miss Terezia Cicelova, editorial assistant; Mrs. Cassandra Pappas, text designer; Mr. Roméo Enriquez, production manager; Miss Katherine Burns, assistant marketing manager; and Mr. Oliver Munday, jacket designer.

Index

ABC of Plain Words, The
  (Gowers), 232
abstract nouns, concrete, *see*
  under noun
accents, in verse, 118
accidence, *see* morphology
Addison, Joseph, 19
adjective
  article as, 38
  comparative, 36, 201
  defined and discussed, 35–8,
    201
  demonstrative, 33, 36
  and morphology, 23
  of number, 36
  order of, 37
  positive, 36, 201
  possessive, 34, 36, 206
  of quality, 36
  of quantity, 36
  superlative, 36–7, 201
adverb
  comparative, 60
  and compounded verbs, 60–1

defined and discussed,
  54–61, 201
  first vs. *firstly,* 55–8
  hopefully, 58–9
  superlative, 60
age of reason, 12, 13, 200
alliteration, 123, 129
amphibrach, 119, 129
anapest, 119, 129
"Argonauts, The" (Lawrence),
  110–11
article, as adjective, 38
Auden, W. H., 112
Austen, Jane, 47
auxiliary verbs, *see under*
  verb

Bart, Lionel, 115, 116
Bayliss, A. E. M., 236
Beatles, The, 115
Belloc, Hilaire, 76, 104, 114
Berlin, Irving, 115
Betjeman, John, 109
blank verse, 107, 122

Buchan, John, 104
Burchfield, R. W., 231
Burke, Edmund, 47
Burney, Fanny, 47
Burton, Richard, 111–12

caesura, 120, 129
Cambridge History of the English Language, The, 231
case
  nominative, 70
  objective, 70–1
Chesterton, G. K., 110
Chicago Manual of Style, The, xxxii–xxxiii
clause
  comma before, 147–9
  defined and discussed, 67–8, 202
  main/independent, 75
    comma before, 147–9
    joining, 149–51
  non-restrictive, 91, 92, 145–6
  noun, adjective and adverb function performed by, 77–82
  restrictive, 91–3, 147
    and *that* vs. *which* as relative pronoun, 92–3
  subject of, 68
  subsidiary/subordinate, 75–6
  types of, 75–6

Cobbett, William, xxi
collective nouns, *see under* noun
comma
  bracketing, 89–90, 92, 145
  and independent clauses, introducing, 147–9
  and main/independent clauses, not joining, 149–51
common nouns, *see under* noun
comparative adverbs, *see under* adverb
complement, 73, 202
  see also object
Complete Plain Words, The (Gowers), 232
composition, elementary principles of, 155–79
  and active voice, 163–5
  and co-ordinate ideas, similar form of, 170–3
  and emphatic sentence endings, 177–9
  and loose sentences, 169–70
  and needless words, omission of, 167–9
  and paragraphs, 155–62
    beginnings and ends of, 158–62
    as unit of composition, 155–8
  and related words, keeping together, 173–6

and statements, positive
form of, 165–7
summaries, tenses of, 176–7
Concise Oxford Dictionary, 47,
64, 86, 108, 189, 221
concrete nouns, *see under*
noun
conjunction
co-ordinating, 62, 94, 202
defined and discussed,
62–3, 202
subordinating, 62, 94,
202–3
couplets, 126
Coward, Noël, 107, 115, 117

dactyl, 119, 129
Daniel, Rev. Canon Evan, 235
definition, 24–7, 203
demonstrative adjectives, *see*
under adjective
Dictionary of Modern English
Usage, A (Fowler), 56, 231
Burchfield edition, 231
Donne, John, 112–13
"Donne and Love Poetry
in the Seventeenth
Century" (Lewis), 112–14
Dummett, Prof. Michael, 58,
59, 233, 234

Elements of English Grammar,
The (West), 235
Elements of Style, The
(Strunk), xiv–xv

White's revised edition of,
230
Eliot, T. S., 109, 110, 112
English Language, The
(Meiklejohn), xxi–xxii,
106, 235
etymology, 27–30
etymology of, 30

false rhyming, 116–17, 126
feet, in verse, 118, 126, 129
Foerster, Norman, 230
Fowler, H. W., 56, 58, 231
Fraser, Sir Bruce, 232
free verse
and abandonment of
traditional poetry,
109–15
poetry vs., 107–8

Gilbert, W. S., 128
Gowers, Sir Ernest, 232
grammar
"cruelty" of not teaching,
9–10
exercises for—or not,
103–4
and happiness, 5–6
main divisions of, 23–4;
see also morphology;
syntax
and parts of speech, *see*
individual terms
prescriptiveness of, xiv,
15–22

grammar (*cont'd.*)
  terms for, inventory of,
    199–209; *see also*
    individual terms
  as unchanging, 18–19
  see also usage, elementary
    rules of
Grammar, History, and
  Derivation of the English
  Language, The (Daniel),
  235
Grammar & Style (Dummett),
  58, 234
Greenbaum, Sydney, 232
Gwynne Teaching Web site,
  xxxvi, 13, 200

Hall, Theophilus, 235
Hammerstein, Oscar, 115
Harbrace Handbook of English
  (Hodges), 229–30
Hart, Lorenz, 115
headings, 180
Heffer, Simon, xxvi–xxviii,
  46, 59, 233–4
Henham, Peter, 110
Higher English (Rahtz), 108
Hillier, Bevis, 109, 110
Hodges, John C., 229
Hodgkinson, Tom, x, xi
Hughes, Thomas, 132

iambic pentameter, 120
iambic tetrameter, 119
iambus, 118, 129

"If" (Kipling), 130–1
interjection, defined and
  discussed, 64–5
intransitive verbs, *see under*
  verb
irregular verbs, *see under*
  verb
italics, 183

Jespersen, Otto, 236
Johnson, Dr. Samuel, 47, 56
Joyce, James, 110

Kipling, Rudyard, 104,
  129–31
Knopf, Alfred A., xi

"Lady of Shalott" (Tennyson),
  120
Lawrence, D. H., 110
Lerner, Alan Jay, 115, 116, 127
Lewis, C. S., 112–14
Lingwood, Jake, xi
"Living Doll" (Bart), 116
Loewe, Frederick, 116, 127
logic, as science of thinking, 7
Longfellow, Henry
  Wadsworth, 123
lyrics, song, *see* song lyrics

"Mad Dogs and Englishmen"
  (Coward), 117
Manual of English Grammar
  and Composition
  (Nesfield), 108, 229, 230

Marlowe, Christopher, 113
Matriculation English Course,
  A (Oliphant), 102, 108,
  235
Meiklejohn, Prof. J. M. D.,
  xxii, 106, 108, 235
Mercer, Johnny, 115
metre, in verse, 46n, 107, 113,
  115
Mikado, The (Gilbert and
  Sullivan), 129
misused words and
  expressions, 184–96
modal verbs, *see under* verb
mood, *see under* verb
morphology ("accidence"),
  23–4, 29, 200, 204
  etymology of, 29
My Fair Lady (Lerner and
  Loewe), 127

Nesfield, J. C., 108, 229–30
noun
  abstract, 32, 204
  collective, 32, 204
  common, 31–2
  concrete, 32
  defined and discussed,
    31–2, 204
  and morphology, 23
  plural, formation of, 224–8
  possessive, 143–4
  proper, 32
  from verbs, 52–3
numerals, 180–1

object
  direct, 69–70, 72, 204
  indirect, 72, 204–5
  see also complement
Oliphant, Lancelot, 102, 108,
  235
"On the Street Where You
  Live" (Lerner and
  Loewe), 116
Orwell, George, 104
Outline of English Grammar
  (Nesfield), 229

paragraph
  topic sentence of, 158–62
  as unit of composition,
    155–8
parsing, 30
Partridge, Eric, 57
parts of speech
  verse illustrates, 65–6
  see also individual terms
period, *see under* punctuation,
  period
Philosophy of Grammar, The
  (Jespersen), 236
phrase, 74
  defined and discussed, 68,
    205
  noun, adjective and adverb
    function performed by,
    77–82
Plain Words (Gowers), 232
plurals, formation of,
  224–8

poetry
  abandonment of
    traditional, 108–17
  see also verse
Porter, Cole, 115, 127
positive adjectives, *see under*
  adjective
possessive adjectives, *see*
  under adjective
Pound, Ezra, 109, 110, 112
preposition
  in compounded verbs, 61
  defined and discussed, 63–4
  special, 218–23
prescriptiveness, of grammar,
  xix, 15–22
Priestley, Joseph, 20
"Problem of Free Verse, The"
  (Chesterton), 110
pronoun
  defined and discussed,
    33–5, 205
  demonstrative, 33, 205
  he, and sex, xxiv–xxix
  indefinite, 34, 205
  intensive, 33, 205
  interrogative, 33–4, 205
  and morphology, 23
  personal, 33
  possessive, 34, 206
  reflexive, 33, 73
  relative ("conjunctive"), 33,
    75, 79, 205, 206

that vs. *which,* 92–3
their, singular use of,
  xxv–xxvii
proper nouns, *see under* noun
prose, 108, 131–2
prosody, 108
punctuation, xxx–xxxiii,
  84–100
  apostrophe, 97–8
  asterisk, 100
  brackets, round
    (parentheses), 98, 181
  brackets, square, 98
  colon, 93
  comma, 88–92, 95–6,
    144–5
    and American English,
      89, 91, 144
    Oxford, 89
    parenthetical, 92, 145
    and restrictive vs. non-
      restrictive clauses,
      91–3
    using full stops for, 151–3
  dash, 99–100
  ellipsis, 100
  exclamation mark, 96–7;
    see also interjection
  full stop, 85–8
  hyphen, 98–9
    and word division, 153–4
  inverted commas, 97, 181–2
  period, 85–8

question mark, 96
quotation marks, *see*
    punctuation: inverted
    commas
semicolon, 93–4, 95–6
    for joining main/
        independent clauses,
        149–50
slash/oblique, 100
Purves, Libby, 8–9

quotations, 181–2
    see also punctuation:
        inverted commas

Rahtz, F. J., 108
references, 182–3
reported speech, 78–9
rhetoric, 7
rhyme, 107, 121–2,
    127–8
    false, 116–17, 126
Rice, Timothy, 115
Richardson, Samuel, 222
Rolling Stones, The, 115
*Rudiments of English
    Grammar, Adapted to
    the Use of Schools, The*
    (Priestley), 20

scanning verse, 120
School Certificate English
    (Bayliss), 236

*School Manual of English
    Grammar . . . , A* (Smith,
    Hall), 235
sentence
    breaking inappropriately,
        151–2
    defined and discussed, 67,
        206
    emphatic words at end of,
        177–9
    loose, 169–70
    omitting needless words
        from, 167–9
    in paragraph construction,
        158–62
    participial phrases in,
        appropriate use of, 152–3
    predicate of, 68–9, 205
    related words in, keeping
        together, 173–6
    as statements, positive form
        of, 165–7
    subject of, 68, 206
    topic, 158–62
    word division in, 153–4
Shakespeare, William, xxi,
    46, 120
Smith, William, 235
song lyrics, rhythm and
    rhyme in, 115–17
Song of Hiawatha
    (Longfellow), 123
Spectator, The, 9–10, 109

spelling, English vs.
    American, xxix–xxx
split infinitive, 44–8, 232
    see also under verb: moods
        of; verb: non-finite
        parts of
spondee, 119, 129
stanza, 122, 129
Steadman, J. M., Jr., 230
stresses, in verse, 118
Strictly English (Heffer), xxvi,
    xxviii, 46, 59, 233
Strunk, Prof. William,
    xiv–xviii, xxv, 91
    on style, 141–96
Style Guide (*Economist*), xxvi,
    xxvii, 93, 230–1, 233
Sullivan, Sir Arthur, 129
superlative adjectives, *see*
    under adjective
superlative adverbs, *see under*
    adverb
syntax
    defined and discussed, 24,
        29, 207
    etymology of, 29
    most important basics of,
        67–83

Tennyson, Alfred, Lord, 120
tenses, *see under* verb
texting, 21
Times, The, 8–9
Times Literary Supplement, 59
titles, 183

transitive verbs, *see under*
    verb
Trevor-Roper, Prof. Hugh,
    137
trochee, 118, 129

usage, elementary rules of,
    143–54
    and parts of speech, *see*
        individual terms
    see also grammar
Usage and Abusage
    (Partridge), 57

verb
    auxiliary, 40–1, 207
    compounded, 60–1
    defined and discussed,
        38–54
    intransitive, 69–70, 207
    irregular, 53–4
        listed, 210–17
    modal, 41, 207
    moods of, 41–3, 207–8
        imperative, 42, 208
        indicative, 42, 207–8
        infinitive, 43; *see also*
            split infinitive; verb:
            non-finite parts of
        interrogative, 208
        subjunctive, 42–3, 208
    and morphology, 23–4
    non-finite parts of, 43–52,
        208–9
        gerund, 49–51, 209

gerundive, 51–2, 209
infinitive, 43–52, 208;
    see also split infinitive;
    verb: moods of
participle, 48–9, 209
nouns derived from, 52–3
past tenses and past
    participles of, listed,
    210–17
tenses of, 209
    defined and discussed,
        38–41, 209
    future, 39–40
    imperfect, 39
    past, and past participles,
        210–17
    perfect, 39
    pluperfect, 39
    present, 38–9
    present emphatic, 39
    sequence, 82–3
    in summaries, 176–7
transitive, 69–70 *passim*
voices of, active vs. passive,
    41, 163–5, 209
verse
    blank, 107, 122
    elements of, 118–23
    false rhyme and, 116–17,
        126
    free, 108–17
    grammar of writing,
        106–32

metre in, 107, 113, 115
poetry and, 108–15
poetry vs., 107–8
prose vs., 108, 131–2
regularity of, 107
rhyme in, 107, 121–2, 127–8
rules for, 123–32
scanning, 120
song lyrics and, 115–17
writing, 106–32
vocabulary, 6–7
voices, *see under* verb

Waste Land, The (Eliot), 109
Waugh, Evelyn, 77, 104
Webster, Noah, xxx
Webster's Collegiate Dictionary,
    xxix
West, Alfred S., 235
Whitcut, Janet, 232
White, Elwyn Brooks,
    xv–xviii, 230
Wodehouse, P. G., 76, 104–5
Wood, F. T., 108
word division, 153–4
words and expressions,
    misuse of, 184–96
Wordsworth, Dot, 9–10
Writing and Thinking
    (Foerster, Steadman), 230

Yeats, W. B., 110, 112
Young, G. M., 110

A NOTE ABOUT THE AUTHOR

Formerly a successful businessman, N. M. Gwynne has for many years been teaching just about every sort of subject to just about every sort of pupil in just about every sort of circumstance—English, Latin, Greek, French, German, mathematics, history, classical philosophy, natural medicine, the elements of music and "How to start up and run your own business"—in lecture-halls, large classrooms, small classrooms and homes—to pupils aged from two years old to over seventy—of many different nationalities and in several different countries—and since 2007 "face-to-face" over the Internet. English grammar has been the basis of many of the subjects he has taught.

His teaching methods are very much in accordance with the traditional, common-sense ones, refined over the centuries, that were used almost everywhere until they were abolished worldwide in the 1960s and subsequently. His teaching has been considered sufficiently remarkable—both in its unusualness in today's world and in its genuinely speedy effectiveness—to have featured in newspaper and magazine articles and on television and radio programmes.

A NOTE ON THE TYPE

This book was set in Old Style No. 7. This face is largely based on a series originally cut by the Bruce Foundry in the early 1870s, and that face, in its turn, appears to have followed in all essentials the details of a face designed and cut some years before by the celebrated Edinburgh typefounders Miller & Richard. Old Style No. 7, composed in a page, gives a subdued color and an even texture that make it easily and comfortably readable.

Typeset by Scribe,
Philadelphia, Pennsylvania

Printed and bound by Berryville Graphics,
Berryville, Virginia

Designed by Cassandra J. Pappas